I0123944

LEADING 21st CENTURY NON-PROFIT BOARDS

—◦oo◦—)◉(—◦oo◦—

F. T. Davis, Jr.

Copyright © 2013 F. T. Davis, Jr..

All rights reserved. No part of this book may be reproduced, stored,
or transmitted by any means—whether auditory, graphic, mechanical,
or electronic—without written permission of the author, except in the
case of brief excerpts used in critical articles and reviews. Unauthorized
reproduction of any part of this work is illegal and is punishable by law.

The NY Attorney General's *Non-Profit Corporation Guidance* is reprinted
with the permission of The New York Attorney General's Office,
and the Charities Bureau of that Office, copyright holder.

ISBN: 978-0-9896662-0-6 (sc)
ISBN: 978-1-4834-0399-1 (e)

Because of the dynamic nature of the Internet, any web addresses or links contained in
this book may have changed since publication and may no longer be valid. The views
expressed in this work are solely those of the author and do not necessarily reflect the
views of the publisher, and the publisher hereby disclaims any responsibility for them.

Lulu Publishing Services rev. date: 11/15/2013

Table of Contents

———∞◦◦}❂{◦◦∞———

Introduction

—∘∘⊙∘∘—

"The 21st Century will be the century of the social sector organization. The more economy, money and information become global, the more community will matter. And only the social sector nonprofit organization performs in the community, exploits its opportunities, mobilizes its local resources, solves its problems. The leadership, competence, and management of the social sector nonprofit organization will thus largely determine the values, vision, the cohesion and performance of 21st Century society." Peter Drucker, 1999

Leading a non-profit board—of trustees or directors—of governmental officials—has always been a unique challenge. There is no financial "bottom line" of profit to serve as a milepost. The members of the Board are often an amalgam of business and community leaders and long-time supporters of the particular non-profit, or are appointed or elected governmental officials. The vision and purpose of the organization is "soft" charitable or governmental work, while the tests of Board leadership are often the "hard" issues of selection and retention of professional staff, balancing budgets, and actually accomplishing the organization's mission in a hardheaded and practical world.

This book will serve as a reference for the experienced Board leader and advisor, and as a general guide for the new

Board leader, or member or professional dealing with a Board. It grows out of a half century or so of service on non-profit boards and serving as a legal and general advisor to many profit, non-profit and governmental Boards and their leaders. As those discussions occurred, time was often short, a crisis looming, and the occasion was not ripe to sit down and discuss the strategic framework and basis of a particular recommendation or action. This book is an opportunity for the author and the reader to spend more time on the big picture in hopes that it will provide a better context for the challenges of board leaders to come, some anticipated and many not yet in view.

No one knows what the rest of the 21st Century will bring as those challenges. Based upon very early returns, an educated guess would include more pressure on non-profits to be more accountable (with measureable results), entrepreneurial, open, effective, cost/benefit conscious, and honestly run. The huge benefit of tax exemption for non-profits brings with it great social responsibility, and, probably, a growing use of the regulatory powers of IRS and of the state attorneys general over charities and others. Experience showed that, generally, both IRS and the state attorneys general were rather toothless tigers in the non-profit oversight area during the 20th Century. Recent activity may indicate that the tigers are growing new sets of teeth. On Valentine's Day, 2011, the *New York Times* reported that IRS had revoked the tax exemption for 72 charitable "supporting organizations" since 2005. While, more recently, IRS has been in hot water for pursuing tax exempt organizations because of their political bent, IRS does in fact play a large role in determining what a tax-exempt organization may do. A good bet is that societal needs and political pressure will require increased oversight of non-profits in the years to come.

For many years Senator Chuck Grassley of Iowa, as either Chair or Ranking Member of the Senate Finance Committee, has championed reform in the non-profit sector. One discussion (in the *BNA Daily Report for Executives*, March 14, 2011) put it this way:

> "Grassley has been the self-appointed watchdog of charities since 2004, repeatedly using the threat of reform legislation to spur the sector into his preferred method of effecting change, namely self policing. Beginning with the biggest charities in 2004, he forced the sector to come up with a host of guiding principles that address legal issues, governance, financial oversight, and other issues of accountability. Through the years he has taken on the American Red Cross, the Smithsonian Institution, the Nature Conservancy, and American University, focusing more recently on tax-exempt hospitals, university endowments, religious organizations, and tax-exempt bonds . . . ."

There is no reason to think that these forces, coupled with federal and state need for revenues and scepticism about some charitable tax deductions and exemptions, will not keep pressure on reform in the non-profit sector.

A word or two about format and purpose of this book may be helpful. The intention is to provide a work which can be read cover to cover for a strategic look and suggested approach to non-profit Board leadership, or as a reference for some recurring issues, and a guide to more in-depth treatment when needed. Some model forms and documents are included in the appendices to serve as examples for the Board leader and her advisors. The author had some success with two earlier editions of a book on business acquisitions which served a similar purpose as both text and reference. Many business leaders and their advisors stated that such a format was useful to them. Those books, like this one, grew out of the need to communicate strategy at a more leisurely pace than was possible in the heat of actual institutional turmoil.

Thanks are in order to my long-suffering bride of many years, Winifred, who herself has ably led many non-profits and has taught me much about thoughtful, quiet, and attentive Board leadership. Thanks also to many clients with whom I have been privileged to work over many years, and to the many board members, chairs, governmental officials and non-profit professionals from whom I have learned many leadership lessons over the years. Of course, I alone am responsible for the errors in this book. I do hope that you will find it both useful and thought-provoking as you develop your own unique style and strategy of leadership.

CHAPTER 1

———∞◦❦◦∞———

The Ground Rules of Board Leadership: Who, What and How?

<u>Who</u>. Let's start at the beginning. Most Board leaders are going to be chairs of a non-profit corporation board. For legal reasons there could be slightly different powers and duties for the leader if the non-profit is organized as a trust or unincorporated association, a governmental entity, or some other legal form, but, in practice, a non-profit board of any size is going to model a corporate board in function and procedures. This means that the formal powers of the chair are usually more of the "first among equals" variety than of the CEO variety. The key formal powers are likely to be to preside at Board meetings and to appoint committees of the board and their chairs. This immediately injects a need for a collegial leadership style, rather than a chain-of-command style.

The "who" for the Board chair is nearly always a long-term member of the board who is recognized as a natural leader by her (and throughout this book, I'll use "his" or "her" interchangeably) peers on the board. With any luck, this means that the culture, process, and expectations of the board and organization are ingrained in the newly-minted chair. It is very important that the chair represent all of the Board, rather than just one faction. The books are full of stories of disasters befalling Boards and organizations when the Board leader represents only a small clique on the Board. The "who" of the chairs of the various committees of the Board should demonstrate many of the same talents as the Board chair, although these talents can be more narrowly focused, and, of course, can be in a more nascent stage. Future leaders of the Board itself, ideally, should have first served successfully as chair of several key committees of the Board.

Selection of the Board chair is both art and science. First, it needs to be a <u>Board</u> process, as opposed to a selection by the non-profit's CEO. The new chair must be able to work closely with the CEO and to have a good relationship with her, but the new chair is not her or her staff's choice to make. Most immediately, the Board transition and retirement of the old Board chair presents the proverbial "rabbit stew" issue—first we have to catch the rabbit. The ideal candidate for chair is going to be busy with many other responsibilities and is going to have to be persuaded to serve in this time-consuming post. In an ideal world, the chair candidates will have led several of the committees of the Board, shown leadership in Board meetings and in dealing with the paid professionals and non-profit's constituents, and will have a real passion for the job and vision for the institution.

The chair candidate needs to be willing to commit the necessary time to the job. The "best" figurehead chair is often a disaster, and the lower-profile, dedicated board member who has passion, vision, and who is willing to devote time to the job is often a great success. On the other hand, it is very helpful if the chair-elect is well-respected by both the inside and outside constituencies of the non-profit. The chair of a hospital board need not be a physician, but she better understand the concerns of all of the health professionals and their day-to-day needs, as well as the community health needs and the macro swirl of change affecting hospitals and their role in healthcare throughout the nation. The chair of a school's board need not have been a teacher, but must have a passion for education and its possibilities, understand the needs and motivation of the often underpaid teachers, and be able to inspire the board, the faculty, administration, staff, students and their families.

A word about the term of the Board chair. I know successful "chairs for life", particularly if they founded the institution. I know a few successful one-year term chairs. But both are the exception. There is a subtle correlation between the term of the Board chair and the ability of the Board to lead or to simply follow along as the professional staff effectively decides the institution's policies. From a legal standpoint, the Board chair will probably be elected by the Board by majority vote each year (and for that matter, can probably be removed by the Board at any time). This does not address the practical point which I raise. If the chair turns over each year, the staff or someone else is probably actually setting policy. If the chair remains for, say, 10 years, the Board is probably re-living the same old policies, like *Groundhog Day*. In my experience, there are exceptions, but they are rare. My working model would be to think about a de-facto term of about 5 years for a Board chair. This allows full opportunity for the chair to place his people in positions on the Board, to lead the development of a fresh vision for the organization's policies, and then to hand the baton to the next Board leader in an orderly fashion. I recognize that this is an unreachable goal for some organizations. A church elects a Senior Warden each year, a Rotary Club has a new President each year, the Jones Family Foundation elects Mr. Jones as the chair for 20 years. Nevertheless, my strong recommendation is that the Board start out with a presumption of the Five-Year Rule for the Board chair, and modify that Rule cautiously and only for carefully considered reasons.

What. What does a Board chair do? Of course, most of this book discusses that topic, but let's take a quick look from 30,000 feet. As pointed out above, the formal powers are probably limited to chairing the Board and Executive Committee meetings, setting agenda and, often, appointing committees of the Board and their chairs. In practice, this is more than enough power to get the job done. The role of the Board is to set policy for the institution, and to assure that those policies are carried out. The role of the Board chair is to make sure that the Board does its job. Sometimes the role is akin to that of a platoon leader, sometimes that of an symphony conductor, sometimes that of a social worker, sometimes that of a quarterback. Always, always, it is a role of bringing out the unique talents of other members of the Board and of the professional leadership, molding them to implement a common vision, and creating the will and discipline to get things done in the real world in order to implement policies of the non-profit.

The nature of the task of Board leader requires patience, understanding of human nature and of Board members' particular, and varied talents, an historical prospective, and, at the same time, freshness, vision, and enthusiasm for the task. The platoon leader knows his men. He knows that Bill is a crack shot, Joe an expert in GPS technology, Sam cautious, and Tom impulsive. The leaders' job is to take these unique talents and use them for success in battle. Similarly, the symphony conductor knows the ego and talent of the first violin, the enthusiasm of the percussionist, the thoughtfulness of the oboe player, the nature of the work played and its composer, and the expectations of the particular audience. The social worker understands the many personal challenges faced at particular times by the Board members as individuals. The quarterback knows that he has a go-to running back that is usually good for four or five yards, behind a right tackle who, if motivated, will be able to open up the hole, and that his wide receiver is being double-covered.

Joseph Schumpeter, in his *Theory of Economic Development*, defines leadership as "doing the thing" without which possibilities are dead. He notes that the basic facts are usually well known. Schumpeter states:

> "[The basic facts relating to any leadership situation] are always present, abundantly accumulated by all sorts of people. Often they are also known and being discussed by scientific or literary writers. In other cases, there is nothing to discover about them, because they are quite obvious . . . it is this "doing the thing," without which possibilities are dead, of which the leader's role consists . . . . It is, therefore, more by will than by intellect that the leaders fulfill their function, more by "authority", "personal weight", and so forth than by original ideas . . . ."

Although Schumpeter was speaking particularly of economic leadership, my experience is that his principle applies just as well to other areas, particularly Board leadership. A Board chair has available to him through the institution's professional staff, other members of the Board, and through a host of other resources, ideas and options and data. The chair's role is to help the Board consider the various options and the risks and benefits of each, to decide on a course of action and to see to it that the actions are taken and the policy implemented.

How? How to lead? There are almost as many different and nuanced successful styles of Board leadership as there are Boards, and it is unlikely that a person will have risen to the chairmanship of a non-profit Board without having demonstrated a style and force of leadership admired by her fellow Board members and others, within and without the organization.

Here are a few observations which may be useful. In my experience, too much of an ethereal, "touchy feely" style usually results in a caretaker Board chair. Of course there are many personal and, occasionally, institutional situations which require both an innate understanding of the feelings of each Board member, and the impact of unforeseen events which have an emotional impact upon an entire Board and institution. But to emphasize the feelings of each individual member of the Board as the primary driver of Board action often masks an unwillingness to address hard issues at the overall policy level. One of the most ineffective charitable search committees on which I ever had the misfortune to serve, spent months with an expert determining and then analyzing each member's Myers-Briggs "type", while the clock ticked on the hiring deadline. The chair of the search committee was so concerned with not offending members and deferring to the lowest common denominator in the group, that, in fact, the process failed to produce a new charitable head after almost 18 months of going through all of the motions of a search with an "expert" in tow every (painful) inch of the way.

At the other extreme, the military "chain of command" style often alienates many members of the Board, and, worse, loses the inherent power which resides in the collective knowledge and abilities of the entire Board. There is a time and place for strong central leadership by the Board chair. Those times tend to occur often at the unimportant end of the Board business spectrum, and, occasionally, at the highly important. For instance, a Board chair must firmly control the routine handling of Board business at meetings. Perhaps a "Consent Agenda" can deal with routine actions expeditiously. What Board member has not sat through the work of a fumbling chairman who has routine business on the floor of the meeting for which there is clearly unanimous approval and lack of controversy, which may have been the subject of long speeches already, but for which the chair refuses to entertain a call for the question and to move on? Similarly, in planning the Board agenda, a good chair should move briskly through the routine and non-policy portions of the meeting, and allow the bulk of the Board's time to be spent on real policy questions and decisions. In fact, a major lack of Board leadership at meetings will result in routine matters overwhelming the agenda, while policy matters receive short shrift as "other business" at the end of the agenda, for which there is never enough time.

In truth, there are times to hear out, and be sensitive to, every Board member and his particular suggestions, feelings, and approach to an issue. Great Board leadership is always sensitive to those times and situations. It may be crucial to an effective Board that a member in the small minority on an issue be heard out and allowed bountiful time to express his view on a policy matter, even though the Board vote against his position is a forgone conclusion. On the other hand, it has been my observation that interminable Board discussions about matters of little importance to the policy of the institution, and which fail to show a healthy respect for the time of the long-suffering other members of the Board, eventually result in sparse Board attendance, lack of attention and enthusiasm by the other members of the Board, increased use of members' iPhones during meetings, and an eventual loss of valuable Board members who simply have too much to do to be a part of a poorly led Board which wastes Board meeting time on low priority matters. Capable Board members will find better uses of their volunteer time.

By the same token, a martinet Board leader who speeds through important policy agenda items and committee reports at warp speed and shows disdain for appropriate questions and input from Board members, will not be able to retain Board members, and will find that the collective experience and wisdom of the Board lies dormant. Such a Board is like a thoroughbred used as a draft horse.

Great Board leadership requires time, understanding of the viewpoint of each Board member, and the leadership skills required to conduct the Board "symphony orchestra" with a strong and sensitive baton. It is a time-consuming task. The time of a Board chair should include periodic individual visits with each Board member, regular discussions with the Executive Director or other professional CEO for the non-profit, participation in all critical committee meetings, and a deft sense of timing.

The Board leader needs an unhurried sense of what is truly important, and wisdom about human nature and change. One of the best examples of Board leadership I know of was shown by a Board chair of a then-racially segregated Southern independent school in the midst of the 1960's racial turmoil. After much reflection, the chairman personally came to the opinion that the correct thing to do for the school was to allow students of all races to attend the school, and that such a course of action was best for the school, even though the school would be among the first in the South to make such a change. Leading the Board and the faculty, students, parents and the larger community to that goal required strong leadership. The Chairman first discussed the issue privately and separately with other members of the Board and the school Headmaster, and eventually announced a special evening meeting of the Board for the sole purpose of discussing the issue, with a clear prior understanding that no motions or Board action would be taken at the meeting. Needless to say, the meeting was well attended, and opinions were strongly held on every side. After several hours of discussion, and the opportunity of each Board member to express her particular view and rationale, the chair thanked the members and said that he would call a later meeting to discuss the issue again. A few months later, he called another special evening meeting and announced that, after further discussion, this time he would seek a non-binding "straw poll" on the issue. At the second meeting, feelings still ran high, but several of the members who, during the first Board meeting, had spoken out against racial integration at the school said that they had changed their minds. The straw poll showed that about a third of the Board remained opposed to any change. The chair again thanked everyone, and stated that he would call another meeting in a few months. During those months, the chair visited every member of the Board and discussed the issue in a sensitive and non-combative way. A few months later he called a third meeting and announced that, after discussion at this meeting, he would entertain motions on the issue. Every Board member attended the meeting. After lengthy discussion during which each member had a chance to speak, a motion to racially integrate the school passed with only one dissenting vote. That dissenting member quietly resigned from the Board, and stated publicly and privately that he appreciated the opportunity to have expressed his views, and for the fair decision-making process. He remained a supporter of the school throughout his life, and, before his death, endowed a chair at the school.

How to lead a Board? In critical, divisive issues, it is imperative that everyone have a chance to be heard, and that the format and forum be well designed for dispassionate discussion and consideration of the issue. Timing is critical. Unless there is an absolute deadline which cannot be altered, emotional issues are often best handled over a series of meetings, with time for each Board member to reflect, and with time for the Board chair and others to consider and discuss the issue outside of the meeting. Usually, consideration of an inflammatory issue is best dealt with in executive session, with only Board members in attendance, and with a clear understanding that what is said in the Board, stays in the Board.

How to lead a Board? In routine policy matters, rely heavily on committees to thoroughly consider the issues, assemble the necessary data, and to recommend a solution. There should also be an advance proposed agenda and background materials for each Board meeting. Members of the Board should be expected to study the materials in advance, and valuable Board meeting time should not be spent reiterating (and reading) all of the content of the advance materials. Time at the Board should be spent on the pros and cons of particular policy decisions and the options available. If there is any complexity, a thorough written report and a copy of any PowerPoint presentation to be used at the meeting should be sent electronically to each Board member in a Board meeting package well before the meeting, along with a proposed Board agenda, and any proposed Board Resolution. There should be a secure, electronic "dropbox" which will make all documents needed by every Board member available online (and for downloading). In a sophisticated organization, this will be built into a secure part of the organization's regular website (or a special Board website). For a smaller operation, I have had good luck using the "Dropbox" site available free or for minimal cost online to store and retrieve documents. A Board member's iPad or computer or other electronic assistant can have all of the information available for use by that Board member at the meeting. At the Board meeting itself, the committee report and recommendation often can be presented in relatively short order, and the Board meeting itself can proceed in a smooth fashion, with "committee of the whole" discussions saved for really monumental policy decisions. Most of the time, even monumental Board policy decisions should come to the Board only after a thorough and regular committee process. All Board members should often be invited to attend and participate in such preliminary committee meetings, whether they are members of the committee or not.

CHAPTER 2

————∘∘⊰❧⊱∘∘————

The General Standards for Discharging Board Duties

Before considering particular Board actions, it is useful to consider the legal framework applicable to every significant action a Board or its leader takes. Members of the Board owe the organization not only the obligation to always act in good faith, but also the twin legal duties of care and loyalty. These are the same as the duties owed by the director of a for-profit corporation and the law is well-developed as to the parameters of those duties. Sometimes in the non-profit context, the courts add a specific corollary to the duty of loyalty, the Board's duty of fidelity to the mission of the non-profit.

The Duty of Care

Let's consider first the duty of care. Although I am slightly prejudiced since I worked in a small way on the project, I think that the best formulation of the duty is set out in the American Law Institutes' *Principles of the Law of Non-Profit Organizations*, Section 315:

"The Duty of Care requires each governing board member—

    (a) to become appropriately informed about issues requiring consideration, and to devote appropriate attention to oversight; and

    (b) to act with the care that an ordinarily prudent person would reasonably exercise in like position and under similar circumstances."

For both non-profit and for-profit Boards, the duty of care is critical. Especially in charitable Boards it is all too easy for the Board leader and member to think that his job is primarily something else—leading the big capital fund drive, providing inspiration within and without the organization, supervising the professional staff. The basic duties are the same for both types of Boards. Simply because one is a voluntary position and the other compensated, or that one is serving on the Board simply because of a history of giving or of family connection, is no protection from the basic legal duties of all Board members, and, particularly, of the Board leader.

The famous and seminal *Sibley Hospital* case (*Stern* v. *Lucy Webb Hayes National Training School et al.*, 381 F. Supp. 1003, DCDC, 1974) held unpaid community leaders on the hospital Board personally liable for not "minding the store" and discharging their duty of care as Board members. In that case there was a Board of about 30 trustees. Both the hospital administrator and the treasurer were members of the Board. The District Court found that the Administrator "dominated the Board and the Executive Committee". For almost 20 years neither the Investment Committee nor the Finance Committee of the Board ever met. Most of the big banks in Washington, DC, were represented with a member on the Board, and millions of dollars of hospital funds were kept in accounts with those banks at little or no interest. The Court held that the inattentive Board members were personally liable for their breach of the duty of care, in leaving the organization's funds in banks at no interest. They were not appropriately informed about what was going on, failed to exercise appropriate oversight, and were not prudent in investing large sums in non-interest bearing bank accounts with insiders' banks.

The "Comments" to the ALI *Principle* quoted above recognize that people join charitable Boards for many reasons other than a deep interest in governing the non-profit, including a laudable commitment to raising funds for the non-profit. "Nevertheless, a prospective board member should not agree to serve if he or she is unable or unwilling, for any reason, to give sustained attention to governance."

On both charitable and business Boards, what is required is attentiveness and common sense, not clairvoyance or super-human efforts. The Board leader should regularly spend time educating the Board members as to their duties, inquiring periodically of the professionals representing the non-profit if they know of particular risks that should be brought to the attention of the Board, and being sensitive to areas which have a history of causing concern about breaches of the duty of care on a Board. Hiring an incompetent chief executive or lack of due diligence for an important hire are obvious areas. Woe unto a school Board chair who hires a school head with a dicey sexual harassment record. I'm embarrassed to say that I once served on a search committee for clergy hiring which was blindsided by a candidate's personal issue which due diligence should have uncovered. The committee asked and was assured that the national church staff would do a credit and background check, and complete all of that type of due diligence, and that our committee had no responsibility for those areas of due diligence. We interviewed the candidate (and about 20 others), visited his church, spoke with references and others and recommended him for the position. Later, as he started his journey to be formally hired, he told his wife of 35 years that he had just filed for divorce, and then he himself declared bankruptcy. Needless to say, he was not hired. The moral which I take from that experience is to always, always, either perform all due diligence under the supervision of the non-profit Board itself, or have positive and credible reports from experts who have that responsibility, and who specifically report those findings to the Board or its committee.

I remember serving on the Board of large school, receiving glowing financial reports from the finance committee and the independent accountants as to the sound financial condition of the school over several years. The school head reported that the accountants thought that we should change the fiscal year of the school and the finance committee concurred. Unfortunately, in the course of all those activities and accounting changes, receipts were overstated and expenses understated, and it was not until about 10 months after the start of the new fiscal year that the Board finally discovered that we were losing a lot of money. The school head resigned shortly thereafter, and the school has stayed well in the black ever since. As the computer voice says at the airport, if you see something suspicious, ask questions and report it.

As a general principle of law, a member of a Board and its Chairman, may rely on information, opinions, reports, financial and other statements of committees of the Board, of the non-profit officers and executive staff, and professional advisors engaged by the non-profit, unless the Board chair or member "knows or has reason to know that the reliance is unwarranted" (ALI *Principles,* Section 325). A Board leader or member may not "abdicate" responsibility, as was the situation in the *Sibley Hospital* case noted earlier. The charitable Board leader should make sure that the committees of the Board contain members who are independent with respect to the business of the particular committee and are knowledgeable about its particular area of responsibility. As in the business Board context, the audit committee, for instance, should be populated with financially knowledgeable members who are independent of both management and the non-profit's accounting firm. Because financial matters are critical to the organization and a prime example of an area in which non-profit Boards sometimes fail to properly govern, every Board member, and especially the Board chair, must personally review and study all of the financial reports, require an annual independent audit (or independent accountants "review" for a smaller non-profit), examine the annual tax returns, and make it a point to visit separately with the auditors, without management representatives, and to obtain a copy of any "management letter" of the auditors delivered with the audit suggesting changes in financial management or control procedures. Some of the requirements of the Sarbanes-Oxley Act apply to non-profits, and many for-profit corporate requirements, whether or not legally mandated, provide models for proper non-profit institutional and Board procedures in the financial area.

The Board leader should have experience and knowledge of the business of the non-profit. As noted earlier, for example, if the non-profit is a hospital, the leader need not be a physician, but should be knowledgeable as to the critical areas of governance and management of the institution. Matters such as maintaining accreditation, compliance with federal and state regulations, patient privacy, financial accuracy, management integrity, proper certification of all professionals, and similar areas should be constantly monitored by the Board and its leaders.

As with business Boards, it is almost as important to maintain the <u>perception</u> of sound practices as to follow the practices themselves. The famous corporate case of *Van Gorkom* (*Smith v. Van Gorkom*, 488 A2d. 858,DE, 1985) involved a strong CEO and Board Chairman who negotiated a deal for their corporation to buy another large corporation. The Board as a whole was not attentive to its duties and really did not go behind the proposed per share purchase price suggested by the CEO and the Board chairman, basically abdicating those policy matters to the CEO and chairman. The Board brought in no outside experts to confirm the value of the business to be acquired or to suggest a formal process to be followed by the Board in deciding on the acquisition. As the last straw, instead of carefully reading the contract and discussing it one last time with his advisors, the Chairman hurriedly signed the contract for purchase in a parking lot on his way in to a concert hall to attend an opera performance. A shareholder challenged the Board's decision in the Delaware courts. After the court hearing, <u>all</u> of the members of the Board were found to have violated their duty of care, and were held personally liable for damages to the corporation.

The Board had abdicated its duties in deciding on the important acquisition, and had failed to exercise the required duty of care. The moral for Boards of all types, profit and non-profit, is that the Board must be careful and deliberate in making major policy decisions. Boards must not only exercise care, but must leave a clear record that shows that they were deliberate in making important Board decisions, allowed time for thoughtful consideration, used experts when warranted, had an unhurried consideration both through committee and in the Board meeting, and have documented everything in the meeting minutes and elsewhere. Time to reflect and answer open questions is particularly important in any such process, both for practical investigation and reflection purposes and for the record. Exercise of the duty of care is 70% common sense and attentiveness, and 30% methodically making a record that important decisions were, in fact, made with care.

Finally, and happily, once the duties of care and loyalty (which duty we will consider shortly) are met in good faith, the Board is not required to always make the "correct" decision, as shown by 20/20 hindsight. If the decision is made with careful "business judgment", from a legal standpoint, it will usually be fully protected, even if, in hindsight, the decision was dead wrong.

The Duty of Loyalty.

The Duty of Loyalty is the twin of the Duty of Care. The Duty of Loyalty is summarized in the ALI *Principles* (Section 310) as follows:

"The Duty of Loyalty requires each governing board member:

(a) **to act in a manner that he or she reasonably believes to be in the best interest of the non-profit, in light of its stated purposes; and**

(b) **to handle appropriately . . . situations in which the interests of the non-profit do or might conflict with the interests of fiduciaries and related persons . . . ."**

The duty of loyalty can be a snare for even the best intentioned Board leader and member. At it's heart lies the obligation to always focus on the well-being of the non-profit which the Board serves, and not, instead, on the welfare of some other institution, or of the welfare of a particular Board member or group of Board members. If a Board member has an interest, such as a business interest, in a matter before the Board, he should disclose all of the facts to the Board and then recuse himself from any participation or vote on the matter. Most corporation codes (e.g. Delaware Corporation Laws Annotated, Section 8-144) provide a safe harbor for a corporation which wishes to enter into a contract with an interested Board member. The best way to accomplish this is for the Board member to disclose all material facts as to his interest in the transaction, and then a have a majority of the disinterested Board members (or of a committee to which the decision has been referred) authorize the contract or transaction, after careful and thorough and independent consideration. Needless to say, approval of any such transaction should be well documented, and the guidelines scrupulously followed.

Similarly, the Board must always act in the best interest of the non-profit which the Board serves. This seems, and usually is, simple enough in most situations, and normal common sense and integrity will suffice. But there are traps for the unwary. Let's take a look at the recent case involving the Robinson family and Princeton University, my *alma mater*.

In 1960, Marie Robertson, an A&P heir, started discussion with then Princeton University President Robert Goheen about a major gift to support the Woodrow Wilson School of Public and International Affairs at Princeton University to honor her husband, Charles Robertson, Princeton Class of 1926. In March of 1961, four persons named by the Robertson family incorporated a Delaware non-profit corporation, the "Robertson Foundation, Inc". It was approved by IRS as a public, "supporting" non-profit corporation under Section 501 (c) (3) of the Internal Revenue Code. This meant, of course, that it was a separate organization which existed to "support" certain aspects of the program of the Woodrow Wilson School at Princeton University. The stated purpose of the Foundation was to improve "the facilities for the training and education of men and women for government service . . . ." through the Woodrow Wilson School at Princeton. The Foundation trustees were authorized to pay income or principal of the Foundation to Princeton University to "establish . . . and support [at the Woodrow Wilson School] a Graduate School where men and women . . . may prepare themselves for careers in government service [particularly in the field of international relations in the U.S. Government]." In other words, it appears that the Robinson family intended the gift to support the Woodrow Wilson School and not other parts of the University. The Board of the Foundation consisted of three members designated by the Robertson family and four members designated by Princeton University. The gift grew to an endowment of $900 million by 2007. Over the years (according to affidavits presented by the Robertsons), the University caused the Foundation Board to fund faculty salaries for Princeton faculty who spent little time at the Woodrow Wilson School, authorized several hundreds of thousands of dollars of expenditures from the Foundation for general University expenses, and called only one meeting a year of the Robertson Board. At those meetings, the four University members always voted as a block and under the direction of the President of Princeton. The Robertson family complained ever more stridently about these practices, and finally sued the University in 2002, claiming that the Robertson Foundation

Board members appointed by the University had and were violating their duty of loyalty to the Foundation, as opposed to their duty to the broader University itself. The suit also alleged a breach of their duty of care. The University Board members justified their actions by stating that the Foundation should broadly help political science and other programs and allied disciplines throughout the entire University, and not be limited to the Woodrow Wilson School. The family and its members on the Foundation Board disagreed. The family claimed that the "business judgment rule" could not apply because the Princeton Board members should not have voted to pay funds to the University because that constituted an "interested transaction" never approved by a disinterested majority, and that, in fact, the Board never itself exercised any "business judgment" at all, but simply rubber-stamped expenditures already made by the University the year before which were simply reported, after the fact, at the annual Robertson Foundation Board meeting. In a fascinating opinion at the summary judgment stage of the litigation, Judge Shuster of the New Jersey Superior Court (Docket No. C-99-02, *Willam Robertson, et al.* v. *Princeton University, et al.*, 10/27/2007) upheld some of the Robertson's claims against summary judgment, and scheduled a trial for January, 2009. Earlier in 2008, Princeton reimbursed the Foundation $782,375 paid to the University for "miscellaneous general expenditures" over the years, and in December, 2008, the University and the Robertson family settled the case out of court. The terms of the settlement called for Princeton's reimbursement of $40 million dollars to the Robertson Board members for their attorneys' fees and expenses in the case, and payment of another $50 million, plus substantial interest, to a new foundation to be totally controlled by the Robertsons. In return, the University eliminated the Robertson trustees from the Foundation Board and obtained a freer hand in expending the Robertson Foundation money for more general University-wide purposes in the future.

The lessons? For contributors to universities and other non-profits, the case shows that, over time, situations change, and funds given for a particular purpose may well be used to support other purposes. For Board members, the case shows that Trustees who serve two masters have a great risk of someone's claiming a breach of their Duty of Loyalty. As part of that duty (or as a separate duty, depending on which court is stating the rule) there is a legal duty to always act in the best interest of the purpose of that particular non-profit. What constitutes the best interest of that non-profit may require a little more thought. A director of a for-profit corporation owes a duty to the shareholders of that corporation to "maximize shareholder value". That means that if GE can no longer make a reasonable return by manufacturing toasters, the directors may decide that GE should abandon the toaster business and go into the banking business or broadcasting business instead, so long as they exercise the duties of care, are disinterested, and are seeking to maximize shareholder value. The Board of a non-profit has as its duty to carry out the charitable purpose of the non-profit itself, not to "maximize value". A community hospital or school generally has a purpose to try to provide healthcare or education in its own community, even if the non-profit could get more "bang for the buck" by closing and re-opening in another state or country, or abandoning healthcare or education and simply conserving its funds for some future use, or by starting to sell insurance to the public in order to make a handsome profit. Thus the court found that there was a question of fact as to whether the Board of the Robinson Foundation had a specific duty to help the Woodrow Wilson School continue its graduate school program and to encourage students to enter the United States Foreign Service, even as other, arguably more pressing demands arose for the University, and even as the University looked more and more to training a broader group of students from all over the world to return to their own countries, rather than to serve in the United States Foreign Service only. Where you sit as a charitable Board member can determine where you must stand on a particular issue.

Focusing the Board's loyalty on their particular non-profit does not mean that a Board, after careful reflection may not decide that the organization has served is purpose and accomplished its goals. In fact, one of the most difficult tasks for a non-profit leader is to lead her organization in the decision to go out of business. Some organizations have a limited goal and such a decision is correct. The New York City non-profit Out2Play was formed to build playgrounds in public elementary schools in New York City. By 2011, it had established 120 playgrounds used by about 80,000 children. It was also successful in convincing the City to start building better playgrounds in the few remaining public elementary schools. After deliberation and consideration of possible new missions, the Board decided to close the doors after adding 40 more school playgrounds, leaving behind an endowment to help maintain the playgrounds that it had built, and to "declare victory" for the organization. The *New York Times* tells of other organizations, including "Malaria No More", "Water Advocates", and a non-profit in England which basically accomplished their missions, and whose Boards decided to declare victory and dissolve the organization. Interestingly enough, the Boards in each of those cases reported an increased sense of re-vitalization as they focused on their mission over a stated, finite life. The Whitaker Foundation, with assets of over $400 million, and one of the largest foundations supporting biomedical engineering, recently decided to go out of business "to avoid becoming a bureaucracy in search of a reason for being".

Of course, other organizations (the "March of Dimes" comes to mind) will decide to modify their mission to include new challenges. But it is not a bad idea for a charitable organization to consider when and whether it has or will accomplish its mission and either move on to other, related areas, or declare victory and dissolve.

CHAPTER 3

———∞◦◦)◉(◦◦∞———

Hiring the Non-profit CEO

From a practical standpoint, no action which a Board leader takes has more effect on the non-profit (and, probably, the well-being of the Board leader) than the proper hiring of a new CEO for the non-profit. While an excellent Board leader can and will make an enormous difference in the success of the non-profit's accomplishing its mission, it is the organization's CEO who is likely to set the day-to-day tone of the non-profit and to actually implement its vision. The best CEO will be a great ally of the Board leader and the entire Board, reporting regularly, faithfully and enthusiastically implementing policy adopted by the Board, hiring most staff, and bringing to the Board new ways to carry out the non-profit's vision and purpose.

The occasion of the hiring of a new CEO can be the result of the founding of a new non-profit (rare), the orderly transition of executive leadership upon the retirement of the old CEO (hopefully, the usual case), and after the firing or resignation of the old CEO (the most difficult case). While the basic hiring process is the same, it is worth pointing out a few differences. In the case of the founding of the non-profit, the new CEO must be not only a good manager, but, usually, a good entrepreneur as well—often operating on a shoestring, building a staff, building facilities, and spending much time in fund-raising. Unless the situation is unusual, the hiring process for the CEO itself is often part of the institution's founding, avoiding a long bureaucratic process, and involving a combination of salesmanship and enlightened risk-taking by the non-profit's founders.

At the other end of the hiring process spectrum is the sudden dismissal or resignation of the CEO. Usually, the best course of action in those circumstances is to appoint an interim CEO from the ranks of the staff (or, maybe, from the outside or retired ranks) to serve as a manager and caretaker while a search process can be designed and implemented. Even if the new CEO is likely to come from the existing staff, appointing an interim CEO, followed by a deliberate, publicized, and thoughtful search process is the best procedure. From the non-profit's standpoint, the Board assures itself that the institution has chosen as good a CEO as is available anywhere for the organization. From the new CEO's standpoint, she can take the permanent CEO reins with the assurance that the Board made a careful, well-documented, and thoughtful decision, and that the entire Board and non-profit community supports her in implementing a clear mission and direction for the non-profit. The ghost that there is a better person for the job somewhere outside if only the Board had not acted on favoritism, should be put to rest, and the entire staff will be more confident that it is being led by the best candidate available. Another benefit is that the organization is able to take advantage of a natural and unique opportunity to re-think the mission of the organization, to adopt long-range plans, and to renew its vision for the non-profit in light of current conditions, as part of hiring the new CEO.

Let's assume a happier circumstance—the orderly hiring of a replacement for a CEO who is retiring or who has accepted another position. Time is important. Too little notice of a CEO change is damaging to the institution and probably should be treated in a process similar to that where the CEO was fired, by appointment of an interim CEO, followed by a thorough search process after that. Similarly, too <u>much</u> notice, too publicly repeated, causes a "lame duck" situation which is usually unhealthy for both the non-profit and the CEO. The ideal seems to be a process of both confidential notice to inside leaders, followed by a public announcement. Usually (and ideally) at least two years' notice should be given quietly to the Board leadership, and about one year's notice to the staff, the entire Board and the non-profit's other constituents, that the CEO plans to retire and that a search process for the new CEO is underway by the Board. Hopefully, the retirement of the CEO has been part of a well-planned effort to groom future leadership, and the Board Chair and CEO have had an ongoing dialog about the retirement date and the CEO's thoughts on a successor.

There may be formal hurdles, based upon the non-profit's affiliation with national or other organizations, accreditation and the like. Usually, these are not too onerous, but occasionally will impose some labyrinthine process. If you, as Board leader, find yourself in the situation of having an inappropriate process imposed on your organization at this point in its life, by all means go to bat with the external powers that be, explain your non-profit's particular needs, and try to negotiate a more useful process for finding your non-profit's CEO, before you start. I recognize that the ideal cannot always be achieved. Ironically, while revising this chapter, I found myself elected to serve on a search committee which will be compelled, by law, to follow a labyrinthine process, and break many of the rules set out above. Nevertheless, when the Board leader can control the process,

I strongly recommend following the rules set out above. Even in a tortuous process, never lose sight of the goal—to find and hire the best CEO for the organization at that point in its life, and to launch that person on a successful term as CEO. Do not stray from that goal.

To seek outside help or not—that is the first question. My experience is that good outside consultants can be worth their weight in gold for the Board and its leader. From a practical standpoint, the Board should form a hiring committee with instructions to bring to the Board a single recommendation for a new CEO. Now there have been successful searches which violated both of these suggestions. Hiring committees which are very knowledgeable of the universe of candidates, are willing to put in the effort and which have adequate internal administrative support, can do the job themselves, without a consultant, but they are rarities

The advice of an outside search firm which concentrates in the area of your non-profit will usually be a most worthwhile investment. In the first place, a good search firm of that type knows many of the candidates personally and constantly keeps in touch to determine who might be ready to jump into the market, who is doing a good job and who is not, and who might make a good fit. The search firm should be willing to handle much of the confidential administrative work required in any CEO search and to assure candidates that their inquiries will be handled sensitively. Your non-profit will probably decide that the changing of the guard is a good time to revise your long-range plan, both to crystallize the vision for the non-profit, and to bring into high relief the qualities and experience needed in the new CEO to achieve those goals. Having said all of that, it is critically important that the search committee itself take charge of the search process on a pro-active basis, and not merely rely on the search firm to suggest its standard template search. Beware the search firm which starts by insisting that the members of the committee take a psychological test. Beware also the search firm which fails to listen to the particular needs of your organization at this point in its life. A partnership among the Board chair, the committee and its chair, and the search firm is the ideal. Usually, the Board chair should serve on, but not chair, the search committee. Often, in fact, the probable successor Board chair is a good person to head the search committee.

The second suggestion, noted earlier, is that the Board charge the search committee with making a <u>single</u> recommendation to the Board for the new CEO. This is debatable, but my experience is that such a charge to the committee brings the best results. Of course the committee may decide to have the entire Board meet several candidates and give feedback. Sometimes it will also want key members of the staff to meet and comment on certain candidates. Sometimes the committee itself will have as members representatives of various constituencies of the non-profit who are not Board members. But if the committee is only charged with suggesting, say, three finalists for Board consideration, the Board will have lost the full benefit of appointing the committee in the first place, and the committee will have shirked its unique duty. I recognize that sometimes a single candidate recommendation is not possible, perhaps because of by-laws or some over-riding regulation, but a single candidate recommendation is by far the best charge to a search committee. The search committee alone has gone through the process of becoming a cohesive search unit. It alone has seen most of the data and spent the most time considering the candidates. It alone is in a position to make the subtle trade-offs in any hiring recommendation.

If it chooses wrong, the Board can reject the recommendation and the committee can go back to the drawing board. If it sends on to the Board its first, second and third choices, it runs the risk of the third choice candidate being hired, without the full benefit of the committee's accumulated wisdom as to why that candidate finished in third place. Subtle matters such as candor, style, energy, confidential recommendations of others, vision, teamwork with spouse, ability to adapt to the non-profit's culture and work with present staff and Board, may get lost in a "flower show" of several finalists and the hunches of the moment of the entire Board. Sometimes there really are two or three or more candidates who are truly equally qualified as CEO, but that is rare. More often, one candidate rises to the top of the list for many reasons and after many months of interviews and consideration by the search committee. My experience is that if the Board chair and Board allow the search committee to get off the hook by simply picking the best three candidates, the institution often loses the chance to hire an extraordinary CEO, and settles instead for everyone's second choice.

Another point about hiring is that good candidates are usually quite happy and successful where they are and are reluctant to burn bridges by throwing their hat into an uncertain and public hiring process early on. The hiring process is as much a selling process for the institution as it is choosing among many qualified candidates, each of whom is anxious to leave her present position and become your non-profit's new CEO. My suggestion is to make the fact of the hiring process and the responsibility and general process of the search committee widely known and to solicit nominations as broadly and publicly as possible. On the other hand, the early selection of possible candidates, the interviews, reference checks, and review of information on the candidates must be a confidential process within the committee, working with its professional consultants. This allows consideration of many qualified candidates, some who may have unorthodox resumes for the job, without jeopardizing their careers or embarrassing the organization. A candidate who knows that he will only be recommended to the entire Board if he is the clear choice of the search committee is much more likely to offer for the position than one who knows that participation is going to become public and might jeopardize his future success in his present job, even if he is only a long-shot to win the CEO position.

The Search Committee Process

How the Search Committee establishes its procedures and carries out its search will be critical to finding and actually hiring the best CEO. Here are some thoughts on building a successful search committee:

A. <u>Pick the right Search Committee Chair.</u> The chair of the Search Committee will be a key to the entire process. That Chair will call and facilitate the operations of the Committee, interface with the Board and with other key constituencies of the organization, be the spokesperson for the Committee, manage the Committee budget, manage the professional search firm aiding the Committee, and, ultimately, report to the Board and make the case for approval of the Committee's recommended new CEO. The Chair should be a long-time Board member who is independent of any particular factions or improper bias as to the new CEO. He should be on all fours with the Board Chair, the long-range plan of the institution as to the direction of the Board, and the role of the new CEO going forward. He should be an articulate spokesperson and a recognized leader with "presence" and respect from all on the Board, and the organization's constituents. In addition, he should have the time available to devote to a very time-consuming process which will involve numerous meetings, potential travel, and much "homework" and effort.

B. <u>Right-size the Committee</u>. There is no magic number for a search committee. Probably 5 to 7 members is best, with a bias towards 5. Sometimes it must be much larger for some reason. There needs to be some diversity on the Committee, not only in demographic factors, but also in constructive points of view on the Board. Each added person has a geometric effect on the time needed to reach a decision.

C. <u>Select the right Consultant</u>. It all boils down to people. Make sure that the actual person from the consulting firm has experience in your particular type of nonprofit organization. The firm should already have contact with a broad number of the potential candidates. For each type of nonprofit, there tends to be a specialized search network. That can be tapped through a larger search firm with many broad contacts, or it can be tapped through a well-placed "one man" shop. The point is that the consultant will not only help the Committee by doing leg-work, recruiting and screening applicants, and helping in the mechanics of selection, but also will have direct access to the candidates in the particular field involved. At the same time, the consultant should be willing to bring in "non-vanilla", "pistachio" candidates, even from outside of the normal hiring universe for consideration.

D. <u>Set a firm Committee schedule</u>. It is elementary, but too short a process will leave out good candidates, too long a process will lose good candidates who simply can't wait, or for whom the risk to the present job is too great. As an example of a schedule which was successful, here is a schedule which a well-regarded search firm, which was acting as consultant to the Search Committee for a new California medical institute seeking its first President, established:

Weeks 1-2

- Discuss and agree on mechanics for interviewing candidates.
- Calendar future calls/meetings.
- Review and agree on detailed candidate and position specification (job description).
- Agree on search strategy.

Weeks 3-4

- Review "Long List" of candidates to calibrate definition of "ideal" candidates.

Weeks 5-8

- Consultant engages with candidates and generates brief profiles of qualified and interested candidates, supplemented by indirect third-party referencing.

Weeks 9-10

- Profiles reviewed and subset of most compelling candidates selected for full, formal interviews by consultant.

Weeks 11–12

- Initial group of interviews conducted by search committee.
- Feedback to consultant regarding which candidates should move forward in process.
- Consultant continues to look for additional interested and qualified candidates, repeating above process as appropriate.

Weeks 13–14

- Second round interviews of finalists with search committee.

Weeks 15–16

- Selection of President.
- Offer extended/negotiated.

Whatever your schedule, it should be clearly established early in the process. Each member of the Committee should commit to attend almost all of the meetings and agree that if she is absent from a meeting, the work of the Committee will move ahead anyway. Consensus is the goal of the Search Committee and will be the test of the mettle of the Chair. That cannot occur unless every member participates and meets the candidates, and buys in to the prior decisions of the Committee.

E. <u>Decide on Criteria for new CEO Early</u>. Very early in the deliberations of the Committee, before particular candidates for the CEO position are identified, the general qualities, qualifications, and experience of the position should be agreed upon by the Committee. The Executive Committee of the Board and then the Board itself must agree with the general criteria for the search. The Committee should realize that no criteria is ironclad and a happy exception may arise, and will be thoughtfully considered. But the odds are that a new college President is probably the Provost or President of another college somewhere, the new head of a school is probably a top administrator or head in another school, the CEO of the hospital is probably a top administrator at another hospital, the new pastor of the large church is probably the pastor of another church in the same denomination.

F. Have world–class administrative support. Just as an army "marches on its belly", a search committee cannot succeed without dedicated and timely administrative support from start to post-finish of the Committee's work. The books are full of horror stories of botched travel plans for key candidates, meetings not confirmed, thank-you letters not prepared, acknowledgements of information received not made, files not properly maintained, a computer data base not up to date, minutes of decisions not kept, and press-releases not properly crafted. The professional consultant will and should provide or supervise many administrative tasks, but there needs to be a clear plan and unflagging attention by the Committee Chair herself to make sure that administrative details are correctly and timely performed.

G. Double-check all references and background information. Nothing will set back a search more than discovery of a flaw in the ideal candidate just before presentation to the Board for a vote—unless it is the bad news surfacing just after the vote. The Chair must take nothing for granted. Does the candidate have the credentials claimed? I do not care if she was the President of X University for many years, did she in fact earn that PhD from Stanford? Is her credit good? Any past legal issues? Do her references give good recommendations? What information do references not confirm? What does a computer search show about the candidate? By the way, the Board Chair should have an in-depth review of these issues with the Committee Chair before any vote is taken in the Board. In fact, the Board Chair, if not on the Search Committee, must be kept in the loop throughout the entire Search Committee process. As noted earlier, it is probably best if the Board Chair serves on the Committee, but does not chair it.

A final point—great attention should be paid to the process immediately <u>after</u> the Board has made its choice for the new CEO. The announcement should be carefully and timely made, those who need to know should be contacted personally or via letter or e-mail early, with sensitivity to the new CEO's present position, and the various constituents of the non-profit itself. The leader of the non-profit Board should personally contact the head of the present employer of the selected CEO in co-ordination with the selected CEO himself. Ideally, the Board decision should be unanimous, and the present CEO should enthusiastically support the new nominee. Key constituents of the non-profit should be personally notified as soon as possible and should be given an early opportunity to personally meet with the CEO nominee. A poor "launch" will unnecessarily undercut the new CEO. A well-planned launch will make the new CEO's job much easier and will speed the implementation of the non-profit's vision.

CHAPTER 4

---••○○◦⟨◉⟩◦○○••---

Planning for Tax Issues of
Tax-Exempt Non-Profits

Obviously, a great hidden asset of many non-profits is the ability to carry on their charitable work free of most federal and state income and other taxes. I assume that your non-profit has received a determination letter from the Internal Revenue Service confirming the happy news that your non-profit is exempt from federal income tax under section 501(c)(3) of the Internal revenue Code (or some other tax-exempt provision), and whether or not contributions to your non-profit are deductible under another Code section.

It is not the purpose of this Chapter to dive into the weeds and details of federal or state taxation. Your non-profit will need a qualified independent accounting firm and legal counsel to brief your Board on those volatile areas of the law as applied to your particular situation, and to monitor your compliance on a continuous basis. The purpose of this Chapter is twofold: first to describe some of the tax ground rules for non-profits and some pitfalls to avoid; and, second, and to give the Board leader a peek at the way the IRS expects a non-profit organization to be run. This is more than a simple tax issue. IRS is, as noted earlier, one of the governmental institutions which actually regulates non-profit organizations. The IRS regulations and "suggestions" in the non-profit area are often a statement of the present "best practices" for non-profits, and are disregarded only at your peril. The Board leader needs to understand the tax framework in which her organization carries on its work, and the process and records which should be followed.

Although there are several types of tax-exempt non-profits, for illustration, let's examine in more detail the provisions dealing with 501(c)(3) organizations under U.S. federal tax laws. To start at the beginning, the U.S. Internal Revenue Code provides for tax exemption for organizations operated for tax-exempt "purposes". The Internal Revenue Service (and Code) state that "The exempt purposes set forth in section 501(c)(3) are charitable, religious, educational, scientific, literary, testing for public safety, fostering national or international amateur sports competition, and preventing cruelty to children or animals . . . ."

Having met that threshold test, the non-profit must meet these negative tests (among others) also:

> ". . . none of its earnings may inure to any private shareholder or individual. In addition, it may not be an action organization, *i.e.,* it may not attempt to influence legislation as a substantial part of its activities and it may not participate in any campaign activity for or against political candidates.
>
> "The organization must not be organized or operated for the benefit of private interests, and no part of a sections 501(c)(3) organization's net earnings may inure to the benefit of any private shareholder or individual . . . ."

The concept of "private inurement" prohibits payments or other benefits to insiders such as Board members or other controlling persons or their families or private companies, directly or indirectly, except for reasonable compensation for services actually rendered to the organization. One well-known Tax Court case involved a small church which paid its clergy based upon a percentage of the tithes received in any year and which had a home loan program exclusively for church members, *People of God Community* v. *Commissioner*, 75 T.C. 127 (1980). The Tax Court addressed the church's compensation scheme and said: "In other words, section 501 (c)(3) denies exempt status to an organization whose founders or controlling members have a personal stake in that organization's receipts . . . . Such is the case here, where petitioner's ministers . . . completely control its affairs. Petitioner therefore fails to qualify for exemption under section 501 (c)(3)." Anytime, anytime, there is a payment or benefit to a Board member or other non-profit insider, the Board leader must "stop, look and listen" to make sure that there is not the appearance, or reality, of an improper "inurement". Your non-profit Board should adopt and police regularly a written "No Conflict of Interest Policy" such as the one set out in Appendix A.

Similarly, the non-profit is usually limited in any lobbying activities or other attempts to influence legislation or any political election. Again, I will not dive into the weeds of the rules, but a non-profit (other than a church), may elect to carry on certain lobbying activities if it makes an election under Section 501(h), and follows the safe-harbors allowed there.

One example of IRS' occasionally mis-guided zeal in this area involved the rule prohibiting participating in a political campaign. In November 2004, days before the Presidential election, the Los Angeles *Times* reported that the Rev. George

F. Regas, Rector of All Saints' Episcopal Church in Pasadena, California, in his sermon the day before, opposed both the Vietnam War and 1991's Gulf War, and imagined Jesus' participating in a political debate with then-candidates George W. Bush and John Kerry. Regas said that "good people of profound faith" could vote for either man, and did not tell parishioners whom to support. On the other hand, Regas said that Jesus would have told Bush, "Mr. President, your doctrine of preemptive war is a failed doctrine. Forcibly changing the regime of an enemy that posed no imminent threat has led to disaster." A few months later the church received a letter from the IRS stating that "a reasonable belief exists that you may not be tax-exempt as a church . . . ." The church raised a strong First Amendment defense and the IRS eventually backed down and apologized. But the case shows that IRS can sometimes take its mandate to police non-profits and their attempting to influence political campaigns very seriously. Blatant support of a political candidate by a non-profit could lead to a loss of tax exemption.

One other pitfall for a non-profit bears mentioning. If a non-profit has 'unrelated business' income, that income, generally speaking, will be subject to tax just as if the non-profit were a taxable business. There are, as you will imagine, a host of rules and exceptions, but if your non-profit uses the shelter of its tax exempt status to avoid income taxes on a business it operates, it will probably wind up paying income taxes on that income stream, or, worse, jeopardize its entire non-profit existence. The underlying reason for the rule is that Congress considered it unfair for one business to pay income taxes, and an identical or similar business not pay taxes, just because it was owned and run by a non-profit. Basically, there is a three-part test set out in the Internal Revenue Code to determine if a non-profit has unrelated business income:

1. The activity must constitute a "trade or business". If it is run like a profit-making business, the activity is probably a trade or business, including the selling of goods or services with motive to make a profit.
2. The activity is "regularly carried on" by the non-profit. An occasional car wash by the youth group or an annual bazaar selling donated goods is not "regularly carried on". The regular leasing of the non-profit's parking lot to the public or operating a restaurant daily for the general public is "regularly carried on".
3. The conduct of the activity is "not substantially related" to the performance of the non-profit's exempt function.

If you do operate a business, try to isolate it in a separate, taxable corporation.

How IRS views Nonprofit Organizations and How it expects them to be Managed

Periodically, the Internal Revenue Service studies particular types of nonprofit enterprises to gauge both their compliance with the law and to help suggest ways to make the law and regulations better. One of the most recent studies is reported in the IRS *Interim Report on Nonprofit Colleges and Universities Compliance Project* which was made public by IR-2010-58 on May 7, 2010. Much of it is, frankly, dry reading. This IRS "Preliminary Summary of Data" gives nonprofit Board leaders a unique opportunity to understand the agency's concerns and approach to nonprofit tax compliance. The "Preliminary Study" is set out completely on the IRS website. Here are some of the key areas examined by IRS to determine whether an organization deserves continued tax exemption:

A. **Unrelated Business Activities**—This is discussed in detail above. The most frequently Unrelated Business Income reported to the IRS came from sales of advertisements in an organization's publications and leasing its real property.

B. **Endowment Funds**—This area in discussed in more detail in Chapter 5. There are numerous pitfalls if endowment funds are not managed prudently <u>and</u> with a clear record of such management. One recurring issue for Board leaders is how much of an endowment may be utilized in a particular year. IRS' study showed that the "target spending rate" for drawing down endowment funds for the colleges and universities studied ranged from 4.7% to 5%, at that time. Now it is about 4%. This is useful information for the Board leader for any type of non-profit because it shows a rate of withdrawal which most Boards believe to be safe at that time in order to maintain a perpetual endowment, and to fairly balance the present needs of the institution with those of the future.

C. **Compensation**—The amount of pay and other compensation paid by nonprofit organizations to its executives is high on the list of areas of areas IRS monitors for potential abuse. Section 4958 imposes a stiff penalty on any nonprofit that pays too much compensation to insiders. IRS permits a "safe harbor" for such compensation by making a "rebuttable presumption" that such pay is ok if the Board or Committee of the Board setting the compensation has a study made of comparable compensation for similar officers, directors, trustees or other key employees in similar organizations, or has approval by an independent governing body which documents its decision process. Here is the way that the IRS Director of Exempt Organizations described the rules for setting compensation for key employees:

> "The board of directors or trustees, or other compensation-setting body, must obtain compensation comparability data for the position . . . . The members who participate may not have any personal interest in the compensation arrangement . . . . The comparability data may be based on industry surveys, documented compensation of persons holding similar positions in similar organizations, expert compensation studies, or other comparable data. Organizations with gross receipts of less than $1 million per year only need compensation data for three similar positions in similar communities. For other organizations, the Regulations do not specify the number of comparables or comparability sources required. Data may be obtained by any means, including documented phone calls . . . . The decision-making body must document the basis for its determination concurrently with the approval."

E. **Governance**—The governance areas receiving the most scrutiny from IRS were whether or not the organization had a conflict of interest policy for the Board, officers and faculty, whether it had audited financial statements, and whether it relied on outside advisors such as accountants or lawyers for such areas as determining whether or not income was unrelated business income.

The IRS guidance is important not only for IRS compliance purposes, but also because it often distills the "best practices" for non-profit organizations. In February, 2008, the IRS discussed the entire area of "Best Practices" this way:

> "The Internal Revenue Service believes that a well-governed charity is more likely to obey the tax laws, safeguard charitable assets, and serve charitable interests than one with poor or lax governance. A charity that has clearly articulated purposes that describe its mission, a knowledgeable and committed governing body and management team, and sound management practices is more likely to operate effectively and consistent with tax law requirements. And while the tax law generally does not mandate particular management structures, operational policies, or administrative practices, it is important that each charity be thoughtful about the governance practices that are most appropriate for that charity in assuring sound operations and compliance with the tax law . . . .

The IRS on Governance:

"1. Mission
The Internal Revenue Service encourages charities to establish and review regularly the organization's mission. A clearly articulated mission, adopted by the board of directors, serves to explain and popularize the

charity's purpose and guide its work. It also addresses why the charity exists, what it hopes to accomplish, and what activities it will undertake, where, and for whom. Organizations required to file Form 990 . . . . are required to describe their mission . . . .

"2. Organizational Documents

[Each organization is required to have organizational documents, including the Articles of Incorporation and By-Laws, which comply with the Internal Revenue Code.]

"3. Governing Body

The Internal Revenue Service encourages an active and engaged board believing that it is important to the success of a charity and to its compliance with applicable tax law requirements. Governing boards should be composed of persons who are informed and active in overseeing a charity's operations and finances. If a governing board tolerates a climate of secrecy or neglect, we are concerned that charitable assets are more likely to be diverted to benefit the private interests of insiders at the expense of public and charitable interests. Successful governing boards include individuals who not only are knowledgeable and engaged, but selected with the organization's needs in mind (e.g. accounting, finance, compensation, and ethics). Attention should also be paid to the size of the board ensuring that it is the appropriate size to effectively make sure that the organization obeys tax laws, safeguards its charitable assets, and furthers its charitable purposes. Very small or very large governing boards may not adequately serve the needs of the organization. Small boards run the risk of not representing a sufficiently broad public interest and of lacking the required skills and other resources required to effectively govern the organization.

On the other hand, very large boards may have a more difficult time getting down to business and making decisions. If an organization's governing board is large, the organization may want to establish an executive committee with delegated responsibilities or advisory committees.

Irrespective of size, a governing board should include independent members and should not be dominated by employees or others who are not, by their very nature, independent individuals because of family or business relationships. The Internal Revenue Service reviews the board composition of charities to determine whether the board represents a broad public interest, and to identify the potential for insider transactions that could result in misuse of charitable assets. The Internal Revenue Service also reviews whether an organization has independent members . . . or other persons with the authority to elect members of the board or approve or reject board decisions, and whether the organization has delegated control or key management authority to a management company or other persons . . . . If an organization has local chapters, branches, or affiliates, the Internal Revenue Service encourages it to have procedures and policies in place to ensure that the activities and operations of such subordinates are consistent with those of the parent organization . . . .

"4. Governance and Management Policies

Although the Internal Revenue Code does not require charities to have governance and management policies, the Internal Revenue Service will review an organization's application for exemption and annual information returns to determine whether the organization has implemented policies relating to executive compensation, conflicts of interest, investments, fundraising, documenting governance decisions, document retention and destruction, and whistleblower claims.

A. *Executive compensation.* A charity may not pay more than reasonable compensation for services rendered. Although the Internal Revenue Code does not require charities to follow a particular process in determining the amount of compensation to pay, the compensation of officers, directors, trustees, key employees, and others in a position to exercise substantial influence over the affairs of the charity should be determined by persons who are knowledgeable in compensation matters and who have no financial interest in the determination . . . . The Internal Revenue Service encourages a charity to rely on the rebuttable presumption test of section 4958 of the Internal Revenue Code and Treasury Regulation section 53.4958-6 . . . . The Internal Revenue Service has observed significant errors or omissions in the reporting of executive compensation on the IRS Form 990 and other information returns . . . . Executive compensation continues to be a focus point in our examination program.

B. *Conflicts of interest.* The directors of a charity owe it a duty of loyalty. The duty of loyalty requires a director to act in the interest of the charity rather than in the personal interest of the director or some other person or organization. In particular, the duty of loyalty requires a director to avoid conflicts of interest that are detrimental to the charity. Many charities have adopted a written conflict of interest policy to address potential conflicts of interest involving their directors, trustees, officers, and other employees.

The Internal Revenue Service encourages a charity's board of directors to adopt and regularly evaluate a written conflict of interest policy that requires directors and staff to act solely in the interests of the charity without regard for personal interests; includes written procedures for determining whether a relationship, financial interest, or business affiliation results in a conflict of interest; and prescribes a course of action in the event a conflict of interest is identified. The Internal Revenue Service encourages organizations to require its directors, trustees, officers and others covered by the policy to disclose, in writing, on a periodic basis any known financial interest that the individual, or a member of the individual's family, has in any business entity that transacts business with the charity. The organization should regularly and consistently monitor and enforce compliance with the conflict of interest policy . . . .

C. *Investments.* The governing body or certain other persons may be required either by state law or by the organizational documents to oversee or approve major investments made by the organization. Increasingly, charities are investing in joint ventures, for-profit entities, and complicated and sophisticated financial products or investments that require financial and investment expertise and, in some cases, the advice of outside investment advisors. The Internal Revenue Service encourages charities that make such investments to adopt written policies and procedures requiring the charity to evaluate its participation in these investments and to take steps to safeguard the organization's assets and exempt status if they could be affected by the investment arrangement. The Internal Revenue Service reviews compensation arrangements with investment advisors to see that they comply with federal tax law . . . .

D. *Fundraising.* Charitable fundraising is an important source of financial support for many charities. The Internal Revenue Service encourages charities to adopt and monitor policies to ensure that fundraising solicitations meet federal and state law requirements and solicitation materials are accurate, truthful, and candid. Charities are encouraged to keep their fundraising costs reasonable and to provide information about fundraising costs and practices to donors and the public . . . .

E. *Governing body minutes and records.* The Internal Revenue Service encourages the governing bodies and authorized sub-committees to take steps to ensure that minutes of their meetings, and actions taken by written action or outside of meetings, are contemporaneously documented . . . .

F. *Document retention and destruction.* The Internal Revenue Service encourages charities to adopt a written policy establishing standards for document integrity, retention, and destruction. The document retention policy should include guidelines for handling electronic files. The policy should cover backup procedures, archiving of documents, and regular check-ups of the reliability of the system.

G. *Ethics and whistleblower policy.* The public expects a charity to abide by ethical standards that promote the public good. The organization's governing body bears the ultimate responsibility for setting ethical standards and ensuring they permeate the organization and inform its practices. The Internal Revenue Service encourages a charity's board or trustees to consider adopting and regularly evaluating a code of ethics that describes behavior it wants to encourage and behavior it wants to discourage. A code of ethics will serve to communicate and further a strong culture of legal compliance and ethical integrity to all persons associated with the organization. The Internal Revenue Service encourages the board of directors to adopt an effective policy for handling employee complaints and to establish procedures for employees to report in confidence any suspected financial impropriety or misuse of the charity's resources. Such policies are sometimes referred to as *whistleblower* policies. The Internal Revenue Service will review an organization to determine whether insiders or others associated with the organization have materially diverted organizational assets . . . .

"5. Financial Statements and Form 990 Reporting
Directors are stewards of a charity's financial and other resources. The Internal Revenue Service encourages the board, either directly or through a board–authorized committee, to ensure that financial resources are used to further charitable purposes and that the organization's funds are appropriately accounted for by regularly receiving and reviewing up–to–date financial statements and any auditor's letters or finance and audit committee reports.

A. *Financial Statements.* Some organizations prepare financial statements without any involvement of outside accountants or auditors. Others use outside accountants to prepare compiled or reviewed financial statements, while others obtain audited financial statements. State law may impose audit requirements on certain charities, and a charity must ensure that it abides by the requirements of state law. Many organizations that receive federal funds are required to undergo one or more audits as set forth in the Single Audit Act and OMB Circular A-133. However, even if an audit is not required, a charity with substantial assets or revenue should consider obtaining an audit of its financial statements by an independent auditor. The board may establish an independent audit committee to select and oversee an independent auditor. An audit committee generally is responsible for selecting the independent auditor and reviewing its performance, with a focus on whether the auditor has the competence and independence necessary to conduct the audit engagement, the overall quality of the audit, and, in particular, the independence and competence of the key personnel on the audit engagement teams. The Internal Revenue Service encourages all charities to take steps to ensure the continuing independence of any auditor that conducts an audit of the organization . . . .

B. *Form 990.* Although not required to do so by the Internal Revenue Code, some organizations provide copies of the IRS Form 990 to its governing body and other internal governance or management officials, either prior to or after it is filed with the Internal Revenue Service. Practices differ widely as to who sees the form, when they see it, and the extent of their input, review, or approval. Some, especially smaller organizations, may provide a copy of the Form 990 to the full board for review or approval before it is filed . . . .

"6. Transparency and Accountability

By making full and accurate information about its mission, activities, finance, and governance publicly available, a charity encourages transparency and accountability to its constituents. The Internal Revenue Code requires a charity to make its Form 1023 exemption application, Form 990, and Form 990-T, available for public inspection. The Internal Revenue Service encourages every charity to adopt and monitor procedures to ensure that its Form 1023, Form 990, Form 990-T, annual reports, and financial statements, are complete and accurate, are posted on its public website, and are made available to the public upon request . . . ."

So What? The Powerful reach of the IRS "Intermediate Sanctions"

Before 1996, the Internal Revenue Service had only a "nuclear option" with respect to improper actions by officers or directors of tax-exempt organizations. IRS could revoke the tax exemption of the organization or not. Revoking the entire tax exemption of the charity was often too harsh a penalty, and, worse, often punished the organization, rather than the party who actually received an improper benefit or otherwise broke the rules.

Under the new law in 1996 and the Regulations issued in 2002, IRS has a much more nuanced and effective enforcement tool. While it may still chose to revoke the entire tax exemption, it now has the ability to impose "intermediate sanctions" on the director or other controlling person who received an improper benefit, and the members of the Board or Committee who permitted the insider transaction. Section 4958 of the Internal Revenue Code now imposes an excise tax on "excess benefit transactions between disqualified persons" and their tax-exempt organizations. Essentially, the amount authorized by the Board to be improperly paid to an insider is "clawed back" to the non-profit and there may be "excise penalties" of 200% of the benefit received. In addition, penalties of $10,000 may be imposed upon each director or other controlling person, who are liable jointly and severally. Needless to say, this raised the ante for Board members who do not stop unauthorized inside dealing by others in a non-profit.

Here is an excerpt from an IRS publication for its supervisors stating some of the recent areas in which the "intermediate sanctions" were considered and imposed:

- Whether disqualified persons have compensation packages from IRC 501(c)(3) organizations that may be unreasonable.
- Whether disqualified persons have received from IRC 501(c)(3) organizations substantial reimbursements of personal expenses.
- Whether disqualified persons use vehicles owned by IRC 501(c)(3) organizations for personal reasons.
- Whether disqualified persons use real property owned by an IRC 501(c)(3) organization for personal reasons; and whether for-profit corporations controlled by disqualified persons use real property owned by an IRC 501(c)(3) organization.
- Whether disqualified persons lease property they own to IRC 501(c)(3) organizations in return for excessive rent.

Fortunately, there is a clear "safe harbor" for Board decisions which involve compensation to or sales of property to or from an insider. The transaction is presumed to be reasonable and not subject to the penalties if all three of the following are true:

1. the compensation arrangement or terms of the other transaction are approved by just those who have no conflict of interest and who approve the action in advance;
2. the Board or its Committee obtained data showing comparable transactions, and that data showed that the proposed insider transaction was comparable; and
3. the Board or Committee documented the basis for its action at the time it made its decision, such as in contemporaneous minutes of its meeting.

The bottom line is not that the Board leader should become a tax expert. Rather, the leader should recognize that tax exemption is a privilege, and that the non-profit must take pains to operate well inside of the boundaries of tax exemption, or risk losing its tax exempt status, and having "intermediate sanctions" imposed. Furthermore, following the suggestions and rules of IRS will help assure the Board leader that her organization is not only well-governed, but also that it has the procedures in place to demonstrate solid governance when the inevitable questions arise.

CHAPTER 5

––∘∘∘✠∘∘∘––

Finance and Investment Management— Endowments and other Funds

One of the easiest ways for a Board leader to fail his organization is to allow mis-management of the non-profit's money. Occasionally this is the result of outright fraudulent activity, but much more commonly this is the result of inattention and ignorance.

To start at the beginning, non-profits maintain their accounting records not in a single profit and loss statement like a business, but with fund accounting which tracks receipts and expenditures for various areas of the non-profit's organization. Generally, a non-profit will have the following types of funds to separate the stewardship of the organization with respect to distinct categories of activities:

- *Current fund—unrestricted.* This fund is used to account for resources that can be used at the discretion of the non-profit's Board.
- *Current funds—restricted.* These funds are to be used only for specified purposes, usually imposed by the donors of those funds.

- *Land, building and equipment fund.* This fund will be for resources used or reserved specifically to acquire these assets.
- *Endowment funds.* These funds segregate resources to be used, often in perpetuity, for a specific purpose as specified by the donors or, perhaps, the Board itself.
- *Custodial funds.* These funds are held and disbursed according to the donor's instructions.

The Board leader must become conversant with the peculiar accounting rules that apply to non-profits. It would be very worthwhile to have the non-profit's accountant attend a Board meeting periodically and explain the theory and practice of fund accounting as applied to your particular non-profit. It has been my experience that less than 25% of most Boards really understand fund accounting, even though they are often quite sophisticated when it comes to for-profit accounting principles. Quite simply, failing to understand fund accounting can leave your organization broke, and your Board unaware of the predicament until too late.

The plight of one of the great seminaries of the United States, General Theological Seminary in New York City (on whose Board I was recently asked to serve) has reported on its website its various financial woes. The current Board and others are seeking to return it to sound fiscal health. In a nutshell, the seminary is located on very valuable real property in Manhattan, some of which it has allowed to be developed commercially in exchange for up-front and other payments from a private developer. Rather than segregating these receipts and realizing that they represented merely the partial liquidation of assets of the seminary, those funds were used to shore up regular operations of the seminary, without attention to the fact that the seminary's regular operations were losing money at an unsustainable rate. Millions of dollars of debt were incurred. The seminary had and has a most distinguished and well-meaning Board. The Board and its past Board leadership simply did not tend to their knitting, and the institution came to the brink of going under. Such misunderstandings of an instituion's finances are much easier for a non-profit than for a business, because businesses know promptly if the are making a profit or not, and usually do not have separate funds which can be tapped to make up losses. Rule one for a Board leader: understand your non-profit's finances and operate on an accurate, timely, honest, fiscally conservative, and transparent financial basis. I am happy to report that, as of this writing, the Seminary is out of debt and much of its endowment funds have been restored.

I recall sitting on the Board of an educational institution some years ago and having the CEO of that institution and its financial officer report to the Board that all was well, only to suddenly receive audited statements that showed a big deficit in operations for the year. The Chairman of the Board appointed a special committee to look into the situation right away and the Board fairly quickly was able to have the non-profit's management steer us back into the black ink. The CEO quickly became history. A few months' later I and another Board member were running a search for a new CEO and were having dinner with a prospect. The conversation turned to financial controls and statements. The potential CEO (a nationally regarded educator) confessed that he knew little about finance. My Board colleague pulled out a statement for the various funds of the institution, showed it to our candidate, and said, "See these numbers (at the bottom of the fund statements)?" "Yes." "If those numbers are not in the black at the end of each year, you're toast." The candidate stated that he now understood finances and would make that result happen. He was hired as CEO and did an excellent job—including hiring a strong CFO and finishing in the black each year.

One of the most difficult jobs of any Board leader is to maintain fiscal soundness for the non-profit while strongly advancing its good works. The great temptation is to go "peddle to the metal" on the programmatic aspects of the non-profit and leave to others, later, the fallout and program constrictions which come with living beyond the non-profit's means. One recurring issue is fund raising for a new building. Donors are stretched, the campaign to raise the funds goes to the limit, and $X million is raised for the new facility. Victory is declared with high-fives for the fund-raising chair. A few years down the road, the finance committee and your successor as chair of the Board discover that maintenance and replacement for the new building will, over time eat up a total of 30% of the initial $X million spent on the facility, and to meet those upkeep expenses the operating budget often goes into a tailspin. A prudent capital campaign for new facilities should always count on putting about 30% of whatever is raised for the new building into endowment to pay for the maintenance and replacement necessary to use the new facility. Just like race horses, the initial cost of the building is only the start of the cost of operating and maintaining the building or other facilities.

Another trap for the non-profit leader is to fail to balance the organization's budget each year. Except in the gravest emergencies, to operate the non-profit in the red, from an operating budget standpoint, is to mortgage the future operations of the institution. Experience shows that there are always challenges for any non-profit. To rob the future in order to make the current year's operations continue without belt-tightening is rarely good leadership.

CHAPTER 6

—•oo◦➤◉◀◦oo•—

Planning and Implementing Tools
for the Board Leader

The Board leader will probably assume his office having had much experience in leading one or more for-profit organizations, and often, several non-profits. The over-arching, measurable objective in the profit-making corporation is profit in the long-term for the shareholders of the corporation. There are other important goals and purposes for the for-profit organization of course, but if the enterprise loses money consistently over a long time, it will cease to exist. General Motors built some good automobiles, it provided good wages and promised bountiful retirement benefits for every employee. It contributed millions of dollars to community charities, it affirmatively helped people of color and others become local GM dealers—in fact, in many ways, GM was a model corporate citizen contributing greatly to the welfare of the United States. However, in the early 21st Century, its board awoke to find that the corporation had lost billions of dollars and ultimately declared voluntary bankruptcy. We all wish it better results in its new incarnation after emerging from that Chapter XI. Whatever happens in the future, the old Board of Directors of GM allowed it to become insolvent and failed the fundamental test of a for-profit corporate Board.

The non-profit Board has a similar responsibility, of course. It must keep the enterprise in a sound financial condition and balance the books. But that is just the starting place for a non-profit, not its highest purpose. A solvent and well-endowed, but missionless church, is a failure. A school which balances all of its financial books and fails to educate its students to succeed when they graduate, fails its essential mission. A charity hospital which is sound financially and highly solvent, but which provides little healthcare for the sick who need treatment but cannot afford treatment, is a failure as an institution.

So how does a non-profit board measure its organization's success and create an institution which is fulfilling its mission? As in so many areas, Peter Drucker said it best:

> ". . . Few people are aware that the nonprofit sector is by far America's largest employer . . . . [Most nonprofits] have learned that nonprofits need management even more than business does, precisely because it lacks the discipline of the bottom line. [Nonprofit leaders] realize that good intentions are no substitute for organization and leadership, for accountability, performance, and results. Those things require management and that, in turn, begins with the organization's mission . . . .
>
> Many nonprofits now have what is still the exception in business—a functioning board. They also have something even rarer: a CEO who is accountable to the board and who is reviewed annually against preset performance objectives . . . ." ("Managing for the Future", 1992; reprinted in The Essential Drucker, 2001).

A study by the Columbia Business School, "The Double Bottom Line Project Report" is an excellent work which analyzed various strategic management systems and tools used to measure not only the financial bottom line, but the social results bottom line. The Report includes the following chart of the general process:

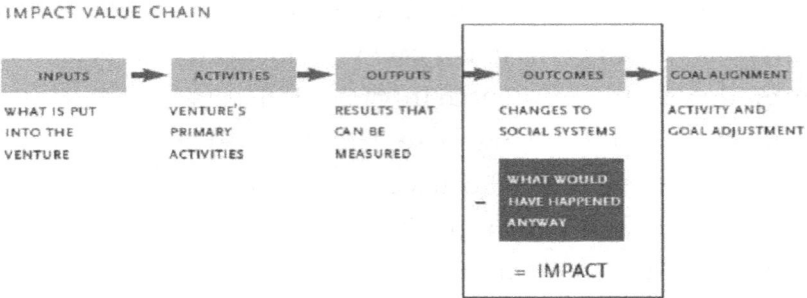

IMPACT VALUE CHAIN

INPUTS	ACTIVITIES	OUTPUTS	OUTCOMES	GOAL ALIGNMENT
WHAT IS PUT INTO THE VENTURE	VENTURE'S PRIMARY ACTIVITIES	RESULTS THAT CAN BE MEASURED	CHANGES TO SOCIAL SYSTEMS	ACTIVITY AND GOAL ADJUSTMENT
			− WHAT WOULD HAVE HAPPENED ANYWAY	
			= IMPACT	

This analysis is a good schematic diagram of the underlying flow from activity to changed outcomes, and then the organizational adjustments made by its leaders based upon knowledge of those results. Many different strategic management tools have been used successfully by governmental and nonprofit organizations, ranging from the "W.K. Kellogg Logic Model", to the "Social Return Assessment Scorecard", and the "AtKinsson Compass Assessment".

An example of dynamic planning and Board leadership can be seen in the path followed by The Nature Conservancy. The Nature Conservancy is, of course, one of the leading conservation organizations in the world, dedicated to species preservation through habitat preservation. It was the subject of an excellent case study at Harvard Business School published first in 2003. The case study is available from HBS and is worth careful reading. For many years the leadership and The Nature Conservancy Board of Governors had two basic performance measures:

"acres" and "bucks". In both the number of acres protected and dollars raised for the cause, The Nature Conservancy was a great success. For instance, in the 1990-2001 decade its revenues grew at an 18% annual compounded rate, and the number of acres protected grew over 100%. By most common measures such as assets, revenues and staff it was larger than then next six largest conservation groups in the world *combined*.

The Board of The Nature Conservancy had adopted this Mission Statement:

> *"The mission of The Nature Conservancy is to preserve the plants, animals, and natural communities that represent the diversity of life on Earth by protecting the lands and waters they need to survive."*

John Sawhill, a former McKinsey partner and government official was the CEO of The Nature Conservancy from 1989 until his untimely death in 2000. The Nature Conservancy was governed by a single Board, but had "trustee" advisory boards in each state and in many foreign countries. With the help of the head of the California unit, Steve McCormick, Sawhill and the Board started an internal Board study and, eventually, a strategic process, which led to a more co-ordinated and centralized setting of priorities. The process was called "Conservation by Design" and followed a four-step process of setting priorities, developing strategies, taking actions, and measuring success. Overall these changes, at least within the United States was said to be a shift from "multiple kingdoms and empires to a more unified republic."

After his death, Sawhill was succeeded by McCormick, who spent three months visiting the global operations of The Nature Conservancy. McCormick returned convinced that the organization needed to focus more on global, as opposed to

United States, conservation efforts. At the time, about 80% of the resources and funds of the organization were focused on the United States, which comprised only about 20% of the world's biodiversity. With the Board's approval, McCormick engaged McKinsey to study and recommend the organization's strategy and processes. McKinsey applied its "7-S Model" examining the organization's capacities and alignment in the seven areas of "shared values, strategy, staff, skills, style, systems, and structure". The conclusion was that shared values and strategy existed, but that the remaining "S's" were lacking in both capacity and alignment.

In true McKinsey fashion, McCormick tackled each short suit in turn. Staff professional development and proficiency in foreign languages were not up to standards. Almost all of the international management took place in the organization's Arlington, Virginia, home office, rather out in the countries involved. Style was often relationship-based and not consistent in major decisions. Managers would simply shop the executive structure until they received a "yes"—leading to a hodge-podge of inconsistent policies and decisions. Skills in the areas of scientific knowledge, conservation, fund raising, marketing and operations needed improvement. Systems were a similar amalgam with over 62 distinct internet URL's, each with a different approach and lack of unified brand message. Finally, the structure reflected a United States-centric organization with some outlying international operations, rather than an integrated global organization. In order to eliminate silos and integrate functions, the structure was changed to a central service "worldwide office" for support services, and three geographic "Regions" which included both U.S. and international geographic areas. Overall, the changes were a success, despite some early failures to fully communicate and obtain buy-in from important constituencies such as the state "trustees".

The experience of The Nature Conservancy shows that a focus upon an agreed mission, and taking that mission seriously, can result in a turning away from narrow traditional measures of success such as "acres" and "bucks". Instead, an organization can change and broaden its geographic focus and realize that fewer, but more critical "acres" may be more effective in realizing the mission of preserving biodiversity globally.

Another successful strategic management systems, used by over 50% of the Fortune 100 companies, by the City of Charlotte, North Carolina, and by hundreds of successful nonprofits is the "Balanced Scorecard"—so called because it balances financial and other goals, and short and long-term objectives.

The concept of the Balanced Scorecard grew out of a 1990 study commissioned by an affiliate of KPMG called "Measuring Performance in the Organization of the Future". That study was led by David Norton, who was assisted by Robert Kaplan as an academic consultant. In their groundbreaking 1996 book, *The Balanced Scorecard*, Norton and Kaplan explain the origins of their system this way:

> ". . . We examined recent case studies of innovative performance-measuring systems. One . . . showed how Analog Devices was using a newly created "Corporate Scorecard" that contained, in addition to several traditional financial measures, performance measures relating to customer delivery times, quality and cycle times of manufacturing processes, and effectiveness of new product developments . . . . [A discussion] led to an expansion of the scorecard to what we labeled a "Balanced Scorecard," organized around four distinct perspectives—financial, customer, internal, and innovation and learning. The name reflected the balance provided between

short—and long-term objectives, between financial
and non-financial measures, between lagging and
leading indicators, and between external and internal
performance perspectives . . . ."

The non-profit Board leader will find that the Balanced
Scorecard can be an excellent strategic management system. To
understand the system better, it is useful to understand first how
it was developed to help for-profit corporations. For a detailed
discussion, of course, the leader can read Kaplan and Norton's
book, *The Balanced Scorecard,* and may want to engage an expert
consultant qualified in the use of the Balanced Scorecard. For
present purposes, the scorecard starts with financial measures,
which are and must remain an important goal of the business
corporation, as they are to a lesser extent for the non-profit. As
Kaplan and Norton note: "But financial measures tell the story
of past events, an adequate story for industrial age companies
for which investments in long-term capabilities and customer
relationships were not critical for success. These financial
measures are inadequate, however, for guiding and evaluating
the journey that information age companies must make to
create future value through investment in customers, suppliers,
employees, processes, technology, and innovation."

To oversimplify, here is how the Balanced Scorecard
process works. It starts with the institution's leaders' adopting
a vision of what they (and those they lead) want the institution
to be. Then a strategy is devised to accomplish that vision.
Specific financial objectives are set. Then key customers are
identified as essential to achieving those financial objectives.
In the case of a for-profit corporation, objectives, measures,
targets and initiatives are set, first in the financial and customer
"perspectives", as they are called. To achieve those objectives,

the leaders must ask themselves "what business processes must we excel at"? Again, specific objectives, measures, targets and initiatives are established for the internal business processes necessary to achieve the customer and financial goals. Finally, from a "perspective" standpoint, internal learning and growth objectives, measures, targets, and initiatives are set. The process is not a static one, but rather a continuous and dynamic strategic framework for action for the leaders, the board, the officers and employees, that is constantly revised and improved and fed into the strategy and vision of the organization.

One example of a for-profit business which successfully used the Balanced Scorecard given by Kaplan and Norton is Kenyon Stores, a large clothing retailer. After adopting their financial goals, Kenyon focused on the customer perspective. The Board developed an image of a 20 to 40 (target age 29) female customer who was college educated, working as an executive or professional, innovatively fashionable, self confident and with a sense of humor. Key product attributes to attract such a customer were to provide fashion and quality clothes that customers perceive as high-value and fairly priced. Included were objectives to provide fashionable merchandise of highest quality and consistency of fit both within a style and across all categories. In order to attract such customers, the shopping experience had to achieve certain objectives, including having great looking stores, and welcoming, fashionably dressed, smiling sales associates. The associates had to know their merchandise, use the customer's name, communicate any special sales, and convey a sincere thanks and invitation to return soon. The same type of process was applied to each separate perspective. The same Balanced Scorecard technique applied equally well to an oil company or a bank or any other business.

But could the Balanced Scorecard be applied to non-profit and governmental entities?

Experience has shown that it can, with great success and only a few modifications. It has proved valuable as a strategic management system, a measurement tool and a communication tool across a broad spectrum of non profit and governmental enterprises. Of course, financial success is not the principal goal of the governmental or non-profit organization and, therefore, the Balanced Scorecard "perspectives" do not cascade down from a <u>financial</u> vision and strategy, but rather from a set of other, non-financial, goals decided on by the organization's governing Board and its leaders.

Teach for America is one organization which has successfully used the Balanced Scorecard. First, a little background. Wendy Kopp is a very talented woman who, in the fall of her senior year at Princeton attended a conference at which a speaker told of the lack of education-major college graduates who were willing to teach in America's most disadvantaged communities. Kopp wrote her senior thesis setting out her idea to create a national teacher corps modeled on the Peace Corps. After graduating from Princeton, and working alone in space borrowed from a corporate donor in Manhattan, she gradually assembled donors and volunteers to start "Teach for America" in 1990—with 500 "teacher corps" members chosen from about 2500 graduating college senior applicants. While the corps itself grew, finances remained precarious and large operating deficits occurred. Kopp soon started two new initiatives, "TEACH!" and "The Learning Project". The first offered recruiting services for school boards, and the latter helped create a new model for school programs.

The Teach for America program grew, but its finances were still shaky. A Greek Chorus of nay-sayers about Teach for America became ever more vocal and, in September, 1994, a very harsh article was published in a respected educational publication stating that Teach for America was both "bad policy and bad education. It is bad for recruits because they are ill-prepared . . . ." Kopp's dilemma was that she was personally stretched thin, the organization was losing large sums of money and loans were coming due, while drastic cuts in program and staff would likely damage the program. The context of her management situation by 1995 is set out in a Harvard Business School case study, *Wendy Kopp and Teach for America.* The second part of that case study outlines how she worked hard, recruited a high-powered and engaged national board which helped her adopt a new strategy. In short order, the board decided to close TEACH! and spin off The Learning Project, focusing Teach for America on its original core vision and mission. The board and staff developed a multiyear plan with five priorities; financial stability; increase core programs; build staff capacity; improve visibility and credibility; and broaden and diversify community support. The board added members who could support an intensified fund raising efforts. By 2000, all of the goals had been met. The board and staff used performance measurements to achieve those goals, primarily focused on activities that they could influence currently. But the vision and mission was larger than just the successful turn-around. After 2000, the board and staff started a facilitated process to translate broad vision and mission statements into a Balanced Scorecard. In place of the key financial goals which would dominate a for-profit business perspectives, the Teach for America chose two "Social Impact Perspectives": improving the educational prospects today of disadvantaged children, and improving the prospects of generations of future children. The new Balanced Scorecard then viewed its plan from a "Constituent Perspective". The organization assigned the first goal, "increasing the educational prospects of today's disadvantaged children" to the active corps members on the front lines. To accomplish the second goal it started enlisting and cultivating a growing group of alumni who had taught in the Teach for America program and who were in a position to influence changes in the entire educational system. In order to equip both of those groups for their tasks, five specific "Internal Operations/Key Levers Perspectives" were identified, which were in turn enabled by the "Financial Perspective".

Underlying all of these efforts were six specific "Learning and Growth Perspectives" which ranged from building a diverse and talented team to enhancing technology. In short, the Balanced Scorecard for Teach for America provided a "roadmap" to achieving the organization's vision and mission that could be communicated to everyone in the organization and those interested in the organization, and could provide a system for monitoring and decision-making by the board and executives. Here is their roadmap:

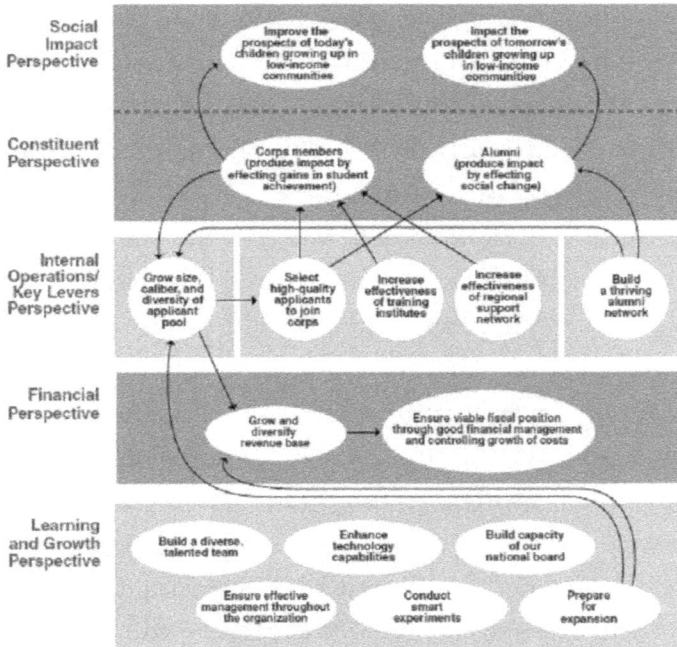

The Balanced Scorecard has also been successfully used by governments. For instance, the City of Charlotte, North Carolina, has used a Balanced Scorecard as a strategic management platform for the management of all of city government. A study showed that the city's elected leaders and professional staff have realized the following benefits:

- Measuring performance has clarified vague concepts like strategic goals.
- The balanced scorecard helped to integrate common goals across departments.
- It has allowed them to set their performance measures into a more comprehensive, strategic context.
- It has encouraged them to narrow their list of performance measures to those that are more meaningful and useful.
- Building the scorecards has developed consensus and teamwork throughout the organization.

In 1999 the National Partnership for Reinventing Government published a study of balanced measurement for government leadership and policy. It concluded:

"Why should you, a government leader, try to achieve a balanced set of performance measures—or what's often referred to as a *family of measures*? Here's what we found in our research: Because you need to know what your customer's expectations are and what your employee needs to have to meet those expectations. Because you cannot achieve your stated objectives without taking those expectations and needs into account. Most importantly, because it *works*, as can be seen from the success of our partners. So you need to balance your mission with customer, stakeholder, and employee perspectives. How exactly do you go about doing this? These are the best practices we learned from our partners.

- *Establish* a Results-Oriented Set of Measures that Balance Business, Customer, and Employee goals.
- *Define what measures mean the most* to customer, stakeholder, and employee by (1) having them work together, (2) creating an easily recognized body of measures, and (3) clearly identifying measures to address their concerns.
- *Commit to initial change* by (1) using expertise wherever you find it; (2) involving everyone in the process; (3) making the system nonpunitive; (4) bringing in the unions; and (5) providing clear, concise guidance as to the establishment, monitoring, and reporting of measures.
- *Maintain flexibility* by (1) recognizing that performance management is a living process, (2) limiting the number of performance measures, and (3) maintaining a balance between financial and nonfinancial measures."

Joe Thompson, a top official of the Department of Veterans Affairs, which successfully used the Balanced Scorecard, stated the benefits of using a Balanced Scorecard for a non-profit or government organization this way:

"Reflecting back on the long history of federal service, I never saw any single measure which could adequately describe an agency's performance. Use of the [Balanced Scorecard], because it balances both internal and external stakeholder concerns, gives us a much more comprehensive, and balanced, picture of how we are doing. The measures we traditionally used tended to focus almost exclusively on internal processes. They also failed to measure three major areas: the real cost of doing business, the impact of the processes on the veteran-customer, and their impact on employees. Use of the scorecard balances our measures because it looks at both external and internal measures. They keep the organization focused on the vision and our stakeholders: veteran-customers, employees, and taxpayers. The scorecard measures provide a 'line of sight' for every employee to see their contribution to organizational results."

The City of Coral Springs, Florida, city council and mayor went so far as to publish a "stock price" for the City on a regular basis. The 1999 study stated:

"The index includes 10 performance measurements most critical to the city's customers (as determined by survey), including residential property values, school overcrowding, crime rate, and an overall customer satisfaction rating. The city reviews its strategic priorities every two years in formal strategic planning workshops. Input to the process is now collected from management as well as front-line employees and volunteers on advisory boards and commissions. Their input includes financial and demographic data and projections, customer surveys on desires and perceptions, customer input as obtained from neighborhood town meetings, and—of course— performance results. Additionally, each employee of Coral Springs develops personal objectives that tie back to the city's key intended outcomes, thus connecting them to strategic priorities and ensuring that they actually understand them. All of these interconnected processes create a city with a reputation for being an open, caring, and good community in which to live and work."

An interesting story of good non-profit (governmental) planning and execution is told by Mark Aesch in his recent book, *Driving Excellence: Transform Your Organization's Culture* . . .

Aesch found himself as the head of the local bus authority in the Rochester, New York region, the RGRTA. He had worked as a Congressional staff member, a town administrator, a staff member at the RGRTA itself, and the co-ordinator of a large public construction project—essentially no experience in running an organization like a large and unionized regional transportation authority. Aesch assumed the CEO position in 2004, and found that the authority had managed to lose $27.7 on a total budget of about $70. In two years, he and his team had turned the $27.7 loss into a $19.7 million surplus, and eventually was operating with a surplus of almost $30 million per year—while increasing ridership, on-time performance and cleanliness of the buses.

The book is well worth a read for the non-profit Board leader and it involves leadership of one of the most thankless tasks in American government—trying to make sense of operations of a transit system. The technique describes, undoubtedly with some paternal pride and gloss, one leader's process to rationalize an organization and to focus on three primary scorecards: "Customer Service, Long-Term Financial Success, and Employee Success". Interestingly enough, it is a Balanced Scorecard technique again, here called the "Transit Organization Performance Scorecard" ("TOPS"). As Aesch notes: "A key reason so many public agencies don't work well—or at all—is that they don't put sophisticated measurement practices in place to support strategy. A school might just measure test scores and graduation rates, but these don't connect back to a specific strategy such as "Preparing Leaders for Tomorrow" . . . Organizations of all kinds in our country suffer from a yawning gap between their goals and the things they appraise in order to evaluate whether those goals are met . . . ."

Certain highlights of leadership described for the Rochester organization involved:

- A recognition that the fiscal budget needed to be balanced, as opposed to assuming deficit funding from the governments themselves.
- Adjusting routes so that service was better for the most potential riders—as opposed to continuing sparsely used routes and times. This involved a "Trip Scoring" measurement for every route.
- Reaching special deals with big users such as the Rochester City School District, that were cost-effective—and being willing to walk away if they were not.
- Modifying union agreements to allow a more rational management system.
- Reducing and simplifying fares.
- Measuring against a Customer Satisfaction Index and other measurements of the Balanced Scorecard. Here is an excerpt from the 2013-14 Annual Report describing the use of four key factors and measurements in a Balanced Scorecard, or "TOPS":

Financial Performance Index (FPI)—35 Points
Success Indicator: End of Year Net Income (Deficit) Projection
RGRTA's ability to be a reliable Public Transportation provider is dependent on its financial stability. FPI shows the Authority's success in managing its finances and being fiscally responsible in the way it provides services to the community. In 2013—14 TOPS, the performance of RGRTA's financial health will continue to be measured based on the results of the quarterly End of Year Net Income (Deficit) Projection, which is an estimate

of operating revenues, subsidies, and expenses across the entire organization . . . .

Customer Satisfaction Index (CSI)—25 Points

Success Indicators: Ridership Growth, Net Promoter Score (NPS). The Customer Satisfaction Index (CSI) assesses RGRTA's effectiveness in providing excellence in customer service . . . . Ridership Growth and the Net Promoter Score (NPS) comprise the CSI, and are the ultimate measures of the Authority's delivery of a quality experience. NPS is a highly regarded measure used in the private sector and considered to be the ultimate measure of customer satisfaction by asking customers 'the ultimate question': "How likely is it that you would recommend our service to another person?" The score is the result of the difference between the percent of those considered to be promoters (very likely to recommend the service) and the percent of those considered to be detractors (not likely to recommend the service).

Service Performance Index (SPI)—20 Points

Success Indicator: On-Time Performance (OTP)

The Service Performance Index (SPI) measures the Authority's commitment to providing the product that our customers want. The most critical success indicator of quality performance for the Authority is On—Time Performance (OTP). Quarterly customer surveys consistently show OTP as the single most important priority to customers. As such, OTP is the sole indicator success in the SPI. Lean Six Sigma principles will continue to be applied throughout the organization to improve processes such as preventative maintenance, repeat failures, and bus availability . . . .

Employee Success Index (ESI)—20 Points

Success Indicator: Employee Engagement

The Employee Success Index (ESI) has a new meaning in this year's Comprehensive Plan . . . . This effort will be measured in TOPS by employee engagement, which is defined as the measurable degree of an employee's positive attachment to their job, colleagues, and organization that then influences their willingness to learn and perform at work . . . ."

By focusing his organization on four basic measures, Aesch turned a losing organization into one which delivered—for its customers, employees and the Region.

A Board Leader can learn from Aesch's experience. Study the issues; develop a course of action; decide what success will look like and how it will be measured, and then implement the plan and the scorecard for success.

A recent development in non-profit planning and accountability is illustrated by the "Annual Stewardship Reports" which the American Cancer Society started publishing for 2011 and later years. The Report for 2012 may be found at http://www.cancer.org/aboutus/whoweare/financialinformation/stewardship-report.

This Report represented the input of many leaders of that non-profit organization. The behind-the-scenes work on the concept of the Report was led by the then Chief Counsel for the Association, Sheffield Hale, and another senior lawyer, Laurisa Curran. In an article in *ACC Docket* for January/February, 2012, they lay out some of the thinking behind this excellent way of helping to lead a non-profit. Here is some of what they said:

> "The past several decades have seen explosive growth in the nonprofit sector. The number of nonprofit Organizations has increased; they are larger in size (both individually and as a percentage of GDP), cover a wider scope of services and are more sophisticated in their operations. At the same time, nonprofits are under increasing pressure to justify their tax-exempt status and the tax deductibility of donor contributions

for a variety of reasons, including their increasing size; the negative publicity that has resulted from various scandals; a public that is increasingly skeptical of institutions; and the historic level of the federal deficit. Donors, Congress, state attorneys general, the news media and watchdog groups are increasingly calling for more disclosure and understandable information about the operation of nonprofits . . . .

The underlying issue in our view is the absence of any practical method for imposing accountability on nonprofits, either to the people who fund them (directly or indirectly) or to the people they serve, . . . [An] effective mechanism to assist nonprofits in achieving these goals is increased transparency to the operations of the nonprofit as a whole, and that nonprofits may use a regular report to the public, modeled on a public company annual report . . . .

The discussion of a nonprofit's business begins with its mission statement . . . . The Better Business Bureau Wise Giving Alliance, GuideStar USA and Independent Sector recently came together with the idea of "Charting impact" *(www.chartingimpact.org)*, and developed the following five-question framework about mission delivery that a nonprofit may draw upon for the business section:

- What is your organization aiming to accomplish?
- What are your strategies for making this happen?
- What are your organization's capabilities for doing this?
- How will your organization know if you are making progress?
- What have and haven't you accomplished so far? . . .

The management discussion and analysis of operations section (MD&A) includes a year-to-year comparison of key financial line items and a discussion of the reasons for any variation between years, This section also gives the nonprofit a chance to evaluate its performance in relation to its business plan. The business section is more focused on mission delivery and related mission goals, while MD&A is more focused on the actual financial business of the nonprofit and its financial goals . . . ."

There is no "one size fits all" panacea for board or executive leadership or strategic planning in the nonprofit sector, private or public. Because financial success is not the ultimate goal of either of those, but rather providing service and realizing more intangible missions and visions, some type of balanced system of setting board and organizational goals, and in measuring and reporting results, is imperative. A 21st Century leader should put in place a system to develop and communicate not only the overall goals, but also the internal and external steps necessary to achieve measurable, short term and long term results.

CHAPTER 7

———∘∘∘⟨◉⟩∘∘∘———

Storm Warnings and How to Handle Them

The true test of a sea captain is when the storms or battle comes. Sailing in calm waters is straightforward, in the gale, everything happens at once. The same is true leading a non-profit.

First, let's look at examples of good leadership in crisis, and then some examples of what happens when leadership is missing or tries to hide the truth.

On September 22, 1989, Hurricane Hugo hit the South Carolina coast and caused the greatest devastation on any recorded hurricane in the United States up to that time. Many were injured and lost their lives, over 100,000 people lost their homes and total damage exceeded $10 billion.

But that was not the only cataclysmic event that day. Two thousand miles to the west, in McAllen, Texas, a school bus loaded with children collided with a truck owned by the local Coca-Cola bottling company, a subsidiary of our client, Coca Cola Enterprises Inc. It would have been a minor accident except that a deep, water filled, caliche, or gravel, open pit was right next to the roadway without any barrier. The school bus tumbled over and 19 children died and 64 were injured. The chief executive of CCE and the whole CCE team sprang into action. The CEO flew immediately to McAllen and told the grief-stricken community that the first concern of CCE and the Coca-Cola Company was the health of the survivors and help for the families involved, no questions asked. There was no attempt to obtain releases of liability or to allow the inevitable legal issues to intrude. Instead, whatever resources were needed were furnished and a large group of CCE personnel arrived and stayed to help the families involved and the entire community. While there were hundreds of lawsuits which took years to resolve, the human suffering in that community was greatly helped, and the good will of the company preserved by the immediate, pro-active action of the CEO.

Again, in 1982, the Tylenol poisoning incident showed how leaders should handle a crisis.

In October of 1982, seven people in Chicago were reported dead after taking extra-strength Tylenol capsules. It was reported that an unknown suspect put deadly cyanide into Tylenol capsules. The tampering occurred once the product reached the shelves. They were removed from the shelves, infected with cyanide and returned to the shelves. Immediately after the incident, sales of Tylenol dropped 80%.

The reaction of the Board and management of Johnson & Johnson, the manufacture of the popular "Tylenol" pain killer, is a textbook example of how to handle such a crisis. Once the connection was made between the Tylenol capsules and the reported deaths, public announcements were made warning people about the consumption of the product. Johnson & Johnson was faced with the dilemma of the best way to deal with the problem without destroying the reputation of the company and its most profitable product.

Just as had the CEO and Board of CCE in McAllen, Johnson & Johnson moved to protect people first, and property second.

They sent out an immediate recall of all Tylenol from the shelves of stores, at a cost of more than $100 million, although it was clear that Johnson & Johnson was not responsible for the criminal behavior in poisoning the capsules on the store shelves. All advertisement for the product ceased.

In addition to absolute co-operation with all of the authorities involved, the company changed the packaging to make it tamper-proof and started selling the drug in caplet form instead of capsules. Through the efforts of management, supported by strong Board leadership, further injury was averted and the reputation of a key company product was saved.

Crises, of course, are not confined to for-profit enterprises. The national United Way and many other charities have had to weather storms caused by embezzlement and fraud. How their board leadership and management reacts to crisis can mean the difference between a permanently damaged reputation and a temporary hiccup.

An example of how _not_ to handle a crisis can be viewed in the recent book, *Waking Up Blind*, by Dr. Tom Harbin. Dr. Harbin relates the story of an excellent and talented eye surgeon who tried to do too much and wound up with malpractice lawsuits for surgical errors, and losing the chairmanship of a major University medical eye center. The events were a tragedy for the patients who lost their vision, for the talented surgeons and physicians who had their careers ended or sharply damaged, and for the University medical center which had its reputation tarnished. According to Dr. Harbin's book, there were numerous indications of poor medical practices and overwork on the part of the surgeon, but the warnings were ignored at all internal levels. Instead of a pro-active approach, the medical bureaucracy and the University leadership "circled the wagons", and, ultimately, some very talented surgeons and physicians were lost to the organization, hours were spent defending lawsuits, and the reputation of a great medical center was tarnished.

Now this scenario and similar situations occur more often in nonprofit organizations than they care to admit. In any large institution, at any time, there is likely to be some incompetence, or inadvertent error, or poor practice which will result in harm to some third party and the institution.

The sexual abuse by priests in certain Roman Catholic dioceses is well-documented. Again, that behavior and breach of vows and trust was a tragedy for the victims, the priests, and the church. But again, a Board leader can take the church experience, and learn from it. In the typical Catholic sexual scandal as reported to date, there were certain "bad apple" priests who, over some period of years, molested altar boys or other parishioners. Reports were received by the priest's superiors, and, unfortunately, were often ignored or covered up. There is evidence in certain dioceses that the bishop of the diocese knew of the abuse, but simply re-assigned the offending priest to another, often unsuspecting parish—where, often, more abuse took place. Recently, evidence has surfaced which shows that officials in the Vatican tolerated such actions by the bishops.

Now, I have been there as lawyer for nonprofit organizations when allegations of sexual abuse arise. These are not easy cases. The evidence is often murky. The Tony Award-winning play, *Doubt*, shows the difficulties on all sides. Did the priest do it, or not? Does the good done by the priest outweigh the possibility of abuse?

Is the accuser free from motive to accuse?

What should you, as a Board leader do? The non-profit Board leader needs to make it clear that openness is required and that the primary rule is "no surprises". If there are serious allegations of misconduct, the leader herself needs to be made aware of them and needs to assure herself that the matter is handled properly and promptly. Having a clear process in place will probably head off big institutional issues and allow resolution while the matter is private and solvable. In the worst case, there will be evidence that the Board and leader did what was possible to establish a process so that a single "bad apple" will not damage the entire institution. Also, having a process and treating allegations of malfeasance, misfeasance, and improper conduct seriously will often discourage malcontents from making charges that are not well founded.

The Panel on the Nonprofit Sector, composed of a Who's Who in the non-profit sector, recently discussed the legal impact of federal laws on non-profit "whistleblowers" who report violations to their organization. Their report stated:

> ". . . The Sarbanes-Oxley Act of 2002 prohibits employment related retaliation by all entities—including charitable organizations—against whistleblowers who provide information on certain financial crimes delineated under federal law . . . . Existing legal provisions protect individuals working in charitable organizations from retaliation for engaging in whistleblowing activities, and violation of these provisions will subject organizations and responsible individuals to civil and criminal sanctions. Because of the great diversity of organizational structure, governance, and capacity within the charitable sector, as well as the variability in state laws, whistleblower policies and procedures will be more effective if they are tailored to the needs of individual organizations . . . ."

Here's the dilemma. If the alleged wrongdoing is confined to the lower ranks of the non-profit organization, there usually are numerous supervisors who will discover and stop the activity. Therefore, almost by definition, whistleblowing will usually involve at least some allegedly improper activity of someone at the higher levels of the organization. At any given time, in most organizations, there are subordinate employees who feel that some activity by superiors is not correct. I recall serving on a governmental watchdog group many years ago which discovered evidence of some corruption in a large city police department, and further determined that the Police Chief knew or should have known about the activities. We went to the Mayor with our theories and he, of course, said, "bring me evidence of corruption by top officers, and I'll take it up with the Chief". We really could not produce hard evidence, just a lot of circumstantial evidence, and the matter dropped. Today that city has in place a citizens review board which could more easily and effectively address such allegations.

The *Wall Street Journal* (March 16, 2010) reported that:

> "Lehman Brothers Holdings Inc. ousted a whistle-blower just weeks after he raised red flags about the securities firm's accounting in 2008.

> "Matthew Lee, a 14-year Lehman veteran, was let go in late June 2008 amid steep losses at the firm as it tried to maneuver through the global financial crisis. Earlier that month, he had raised concerns with Lehman's auditor, Ernst & Young, that the securities firm was temporarily moving $50 billion in assets off its balance sheet.

"This accounting strategy helped to mask the risks Lehman was taking amid scrutiny by investors and regulators about the health of Wall Street firms."

Obviously, human nature being what it is, the list could go on. What should the Board leader really do?

First, realize that early identification of a real issue is a blessing to the organization. You must let other Board members and all of the professional staff know that you and the Board are serious—"no surprises". Often, you can resolve a matter easily when it is in the bud. After you add delay and attempts to hide an issue, wrongdoing which seems small can seriously damage any organization and be irretrievably harmful to those involved.

Second, realize that human nature is such that the whistleblower may have his own agenda, and that there must be a set process which is followed. This keeps things impartial, and also lets a whistleblower raising unfounded charges know that he will be uncovered for what he is through the investigation.

Third, have a published process, known to all, and accessible through a non-line position, such as the outside or inside counsel for the organization. If the charge is serious enough, and the evidence credible, the regular counsel should then engage special, unaffiliated counsel to investigate and report to the Board (under the umbrella of attorney-client privilege). Get the answer straight, get it right and get it fast.

CHAPTER 8

———∘∘∘)❀(∘∘∘———

Concluding Thoughts on Leadership of Non-Profit Boards

The goal of this book is not to provide the leader with a "cookbook" to follow in leading your non-profit organizations. You were not selected as leader to follow any rigid guidelines or someone else's model. You were selected to lead in order to deal with dynamic and original situations as they develop, and to leave the organization a stronger and better one for your having held the reins for a while. Yet the approach in this book can be of immense help as you refine and improve on the techniques and methods discussed in this book.

The work that your organization does is undoubtedly quite important and makes a great contribution to making your corner of the world a better place. That is the reason you are the organization's leader, after all. Your term in office will be fleeting, and the minutiae of the organization will push back against making any real change or setting out in a new strategic direction.

In a former life I headed a federal study of all of the law enforcement and investigative agencies of the United States. I remember when we looked at the appointment book of a former head of the FBI. He had been appointed and confirmed with great hope. He was one of the most qualified FBI Directors ever to take office. But a post-mortem of his appointment calendar for the first 6 months of his term showed that the Bureau staff had sent him on a never-ending swirl of ribbon-cuttings, visits to far-away FBI offices, appearances at important sounding international meetings, and generally, doing anything other than planning and implementing a new strategic direction for the Bureau. In any organization there are entrenched forces which want no change and will fight to preserve the present way of doing things. The organizational motivation is not necessarily malevolent. It is often a legitimate desire of everyone in a far-flung empire to see the new emperor. Everyone wants a piece of the new leader. Intentional or not, a bureaucracy could not come up with a better way to deter a leader from focusing on strategic change than scheduling urgent, but unimportant matters for every waking hour of the leader's day.

You as leader need to know your own mind. You must take time to learn and to listen and to understand. To paraphrase Reinhold Niebuhr, you should accept the things you cannot change; have courage to change the things you can and should; and have the wisdom to know the difference.

To return to the place we started, your unique task as leader of a non-profit Board is to draw out the talents of every member of the Board. You should be the symphony conductor—helping to choose the works to be played, picking the best available talent for each part, and then setting the strategic direction and tactics to conduct a masterpiece. If the founders of the organization had wanted governance by dictator, they would not have created a Board. If they had wished the Board to be an unco-ordinated gaggle of members, each pulling in a different direction, they would not have provided for your position as Board chair.

Finally, remember that you have been given a great gift and opportunity which few have. You, as Board leader, have the opportunity to cause the Board to set the course for your institution for years to come, to achieve things which the organization has never achieved before—to serve, and to leave your organization stronger and better than you found it.

APPENDIX A

———∞⦿∞———

IRS: Sample Conflict of Interest Policy

Article I
Purpose

The purpose of the conflict of interest policy is to protect this tax-exempt organization's (Organization) interest when it is contemplating entering into a transaction or arrangement that might benefit the private interest of an officer or director of the Organization or might result in a possible excess benefit transaction. This policy is intended to supplement but not replace any applicable state and federal laws governing conflict of interest applicable to nonprofit and charitable organizations.

Article II
Definitions

1. Interested Person

Any director, principal officer, or member of a committee with governing board delegated powers, who has a direct or indirect financial interest, as defined below, is an interested person.

2. Financial Interest

A person has a financial interest if the person has, directly or indirectly, through business, investment, or family:

    a. An ownership or investment interest in any entity with which the Organization has a transaction or arrangement,

    b. A compensation arrangement with the Organization or with any entity or individual with which the Organization has a transaction or arrangement, or

    c. A potential ownership or investment interest in, or compensation arrangement with, any entity or individual with which the Organization is negotiating a transaction or arrangement.

Compensation includes direct and indirect remuneration as well as gifts or favors that are not insubstantial.

A financial interest is not necessarily a conflict of interest. Under Article III, Section 2, a person who has a financial interest may have a conflict of interest only if the appropriate governing board or committee decides that a conflict of interest exists.

Article III
Procedures

1. Duty to Disclose

In connection with any actual or possible conflict of interest, an interested person must disclose the existence of the financial interest and be given the opportunity to disclose all material facts to the directors and members of committees with governing board delegated powers considering the proposed transaction or arrangement.

2. **Determining Whether a Conflict of Interest Exists**

After disclosure of the financial interest and all material facts, and after any discussion with the interested person, s/he shall leave the governing board or committee meeting while the determination of a conflict of interest is discussed and voted upon. The remaining board or committee members shall decide if a conflict of interest exists.

3. **Procedures for Addressing the Conflict of Interest**

a. An interested person may make a presentation at the governing board or committee meeting, but after the presentation, s/he shall leave the meeting during the discussion of, and the vote on, the transaction or arrangement involving the possible conflict of interest.

b. The chairperson of the governing board or committee shall, if appropriate, appoint a disinterested person or committee to investigate alternatives to the proposed transaction or arrangement.

c. After exercising due diligence, the governing board or committee shall determine whether the Organization can obtain with reasonable efforts a more advantageous transaction or arrangement from a person or entity that would not give rise to a conflict of interest.

d. If a more advantageous transaction or arrangement is not reasonably possible under circumstances not producing a conflict of interest, the governing board or committee shall determine by a majority vote of the disinterested directors whether the transaction or arrangement is in the Organization's best interest, for its own benefit, and whether it is fair and reasonable. In conformity with the above determination, it shall make its decision as to whether to enter into the transaction or arrangement.

4. Violations of the Conflicts of Interest Policy

a. If the governing board or committee has reasonable cause to believe a member has failed to disclose actual or possible conflicts of interest, it shall inform the member of the basis for such belief and afford the member an opportunity to explain the alleged failure to disclose.

b. If, after hearing the member's response and after making further investigation as warranted by the circumstances, the governing board or committee determines the member has failed to disclose an actual or possible conflict of interest, it shall take appropriate disciplinary and corrective action.

Article IV
Records of Proceedings

The minutes of the governing board and all committees with board delegated powers shall contain:

a. The names of the persons who disclosed or otherwise were found to have a financial interest in connection with an actual or possible conflict of interest, the nature of the financial interest, any action taken to determine whether a conflict of interest was present, and the governing board's or committee's decision as to whether a conflict of interest in fact existed.

b. The names of the persons who were present for discussions and votes relating to the transaction or arrangement, the content of the discussion, including any alternatives to the proposed transaction or arrangement, and a record of any votes taken in connection with the proceedings.

Article V
Compensation

a. A voting member of the governing board who receives compensation, directly or indirectly, from the Organization for services is precluded from voting on matters pertaining to that member's compensation.

b. A voting member of any committee whose jurisdiction includes compensation matters and who receives compensation, directly or indirectly, from the Organization for services is precluded from voting on matters pertaining to that member's compensation.

c. No voting member of the governing board or any committee whose jurisdiction includes compensation matters and who receives compensation, directly or indirectly, from the Organization, either individually or collectively, is prohibited from providing information to any committee regarding compensation.

Article VI
Annual Statements

Each director, principal officer and member of a committee with governing board delegated powers shall annually sign a statement which affirms such person:

a. Has received a copy of the conflicts of interest policy,

b. Has read and understands the policy,

c. Has agreed to comply with the policy, and

d. Understands the Organization is charitable and in order to maintain its federal tax exemption, it must engage primarily in activities which accomplish one or more of its tax-exempt purposes.

Article VII
Periodic Reviews

To ensure the Organization operates in a manner consistent with charitable purposes and does not engage in activities that could jeopardize its tax-exempt status, periodic reviews shall be conducted. The periodic reviews shall, at a minimum, include the following subjects:

a. Whether compensation arrangements and benefits are reasonable, based on competent survey information, and the result of arm's length bargaining,

b. Whether partnerships, joint ventures, and arrangements with management organizations conform to the Organization's written policies, are properly recorded, reflect reasonable investment or payments for goods and services, further charitable purposes and do not result in inurement, impermissible private benefit or in an excess benefit transaction.

Article VIII
Use of Outside Experts

When conducting the periodic reviews as provided for in Article VII, the Organization may, but need not, use outside advisors. If outside experts are used, their use shall not relieve the governing board of its responsibility for ensuring periodic reviews are conducted."

APPENDIX B

———∘∘◦❧◦∘∘———

Form of By Laws for a Non-Profit Corporation formed to Run an International Convention

BYLAWS

OF

NON PROFIT CORPORATION

a Georgia Nonprofit Corporation

ARTICLE I
OFFICES

Section 1.1 Principal Office. This corporation's initial principal office shall be at 100 Main Street Avenue, Suite 50, Atlanta, Georgia. The Board of Directors of this corporation (the "Board") is granted full power and authority to change such office and the corporation's registered office at any time.

Section 1.2 Other Offices. Branch or subordinate offices may be established at any time by the Board at any place or places.

ARTICLE II
PURPOSES

Section 2.1 Purposes. The specific and primary purposes of this corporation are charitable and public, meeting the requirements for exemption under Section 501(c)(4) of the Internal Revenue Code of 1986, namely, to promote social welfare of the communities in which Bigfoot Organization serves, and specifically to serve as the organizing and host entity for the Non Profit Convention to facilitate and coordinate the charitable and humanitarian activities of the Non Profit and its member clubs. This corporation shall not carry out any activities which are not in furtherance of these specific purposes or any activity prohibited to an organization exempt from federal income taxation under said Section 501(c)(4).

ARTICLE III
MEMBERSHIP

Section 3.1 No Members. This corporation shall have no members. Any action for which there is no specific provision in the Georgia Nonprofit Corporation Code applicable to a corporation which has no members and which would otherwise require approval by a majority of all members or approval by the members shall require only approval of the Board. All rights that would otherwise vest in the members shall vest in the directors.

Section 3.2 Associates. Nothing in this Article III shall be construed as limiting the right of this corporation to refer to persons associated with it as "members" even though such persons are not members.

ARTICLE IV
DIRECTORS

Section 4.1 Powers of Directors. Subject to the limitations of the Articles and these Bylaws, the activities and affairs of this corporation shall be conducted and all corporate powers shall be exercised by or under the direction of the Board. The Board may delegate the management of the activities of this corporation to any person or persons or committees however composed, provided that the activities and affairs of this corporation shall be managed and all corporate powers shall be exercised under the ultimate direction of the Board. Without prejudice to such general powers, but subject to the same limitations, it is hereby expressly declared that the Board shall have the following powers in addition to the other powers enumerated in these Bylaws:

    (a) To select and remove all the other officers, agents, committee members, and employees of this corporation, prescribe powers and duties for them as may not be inconsistent with law, the Articles or these Bylaws, fix their compensation and require from them security for faithful service.

    (b) To conduct, manage and control the affairs and activities of this corporation and to make such rules and regulations therefor not inconsistent with law, the Articles or these Bylaws, as they may deem appropriate.

(c) To adopt, make and use a corporate seal, and to alter the form of such seal from time to time as they may deem appropriate.

(d) To borrow money and incur indebtedness for the purposes of this corporation, and to cause to be executed and delivered therefor, in the corporate name, promissory notes, bonds, debentures, deeds of trust, mortgages, pledges, hypothecations, or other evidences of debt and securities therefor.

Section 4.2 Number and Term of Directors. The authorized number of directors shall consist of three (3) or more directors, with the exact number to be fixed by resolution of the Board from time to time. The original directors shall be appointed by written Consent of the Incorporator, and shall thereafter be elected by a majority of the members of the Board then holding office, each to serve at the pleasure of the Board.

Section 4.3 Selection And Term Of Office of HC members. A Host Committee ("HC") shall be formed as a standing advisory committee of this corporation to advise the Board of Directors and to assist the Board in managing and coordinating the activities of the corporation in preparing for the Non Profit Convention. The Host Committee shall be appointed by the Board from time to time to serve at the pleasure of the Board. The Board shall have the power to remove any person from the HC with or without cause, and to select a replacement to serve in that position, by majority vote of the directors then in office. Upon any such removal, the person who is removed shall cease to be a HC member, and any replacement who is appointed to fill that position thereupon also shall serve as an HC member.

Section 4.4 Vacancies.

(a) Any director may resign effective upon giving written notice to the Chairman of the Board, the Vice Chairman, the Secretary or the Board itself, unless the notice specifies a later time for the effectiveness of such resignation. If the resignation is effective at a future time, a successor may be selected before such time, to take office when the resignation becomes effective.

(b) Any vacancy in the Board may be filled by the Board's appointment of a successor to fill the designated office. Each director so selected shall hold office at the pleasure of the Board.

ARTICLE V
MEETINGS OF THE BOARD

Section 5.1 Place Of Meeting. Meetings of the Board shall be held at any place within or without the State of Georgia which has been designated from time to time by the Board. In the absence of such designation, regular meetings shall be held at the principal office of this corporation.

Section 5.2 Annual Meetings. The Board shall hold an annual meeting for the purpose of organization, selection of any directors and officers and the transaction of other business.

Section 5.3 Regular Meetings. Regular meetings of the Board shall be held without call or notice on such dates and at such times as may be fixed from time to time by the Board.

Section 5.4 Special Meetings.

(a) Special meetings of the Board for any purpose or purposes may be called at any time by the Chairman of the Board, the Vice Chairman, the Secretary, or any two directors. Special meetings of the Board shall be held upon four days' notice by first-class mail or 48 hours' notice given personally or by telephone, telecopy, telegraph, telex, e-mail or other similar means of communication. Any such notice shall be addressed or delivered to each director at such director's address as it is shown upon the records of this corporation or as may have been given to this corporation by the director for purposes of notice or, if such address is not shown on such records or is not readily ascertainable, at the place in which the meetings of the directors are regularly held.

(b) Notice by mail shall be deemed to have been given at the time a written notice is deposited in the United States mails, postage prepaid, with copy via e-mail. Any other written notice shall be deemed to have been given at the time it is personally delivered to the recipient or is delivered to a common carrier for transmission, or actually transmitted by the person giving the notice by electronic means, to the recipient. Oral notice shall be deemed to have been given at the time it is communicated, in person or by telephone or wireless, to the recipient or to a person at the office of the recipient who the person giving the notice has reason to believe will promptly communicate it to the receiver.

Section 5.5 Quorum. A majority of the members of the Board then holding office constitutes a quorum of the Board for the transaction of business

Section 5.6 Voting. Each director present shall be entitled to one vote on each matter placed before a meeting.

Section 5.7 Participation In Meetings By Conference Telephone. Members of the Board may participate in a meeting through use of conference telephone or similar communications equipment, so long as all members participating in such meeting can hear one another.

Section 5.8 Waiver Of Notice. Notice of a meeting need not be given to any director who signs a waiver of notice or a written consent to holding the meeting or an approval of the minutes thereof, whether before or after the meeting, or who attends the meeting without protesting, prior thereto or at its commencement, the lack of notice to such director.

Section 5.9 Action Without Meeting. Any action required or permitted to be taken by the Board may be taken without a meeting, if all members of the Board shall individually or collectively consent in writing to such action. Such consent or consents shall have the same effect as a unanimous vote of the Board and shall be filed with the minutes of the proceedings of the Board. For purposes of this Section 5.9 only, "all members of the Board" shall not include any "interested director".

Section 5.10 Adjournment. A majority of the directors present, whether or not a quorum is present, may adjourn any directors' meeting to another time and place. Notice of the time and place of holding an adjourned meeting need not be given to absent directors if the time and place be fixed at the meeting adjourned

Section 5.11 Rights Of Inspection. Each director of this corporation shall have the absolute right at any reasonable time to inspect and copy all books, records and documents of every kind and to inspect the physical properties of this corporation.

Section 5.12 Board Committees.

(a) The Board may appoint one or more committees, each consisting of two or more directors, and delegate to such committees any of the authority of the Board, except with respect to:

(1) The approval of any action for which the Georgia Nonprofit Corporation Code requires approval of the Board;

(2) The filling of vacancies on the Board or on any committee;

(3) The fixing of compensation of the directors for serving on the Board or any committee;

(4) The amendment or repeal of bylaws or articles or the adoption of new bylaws or articles;

(5) The amendment or repeal of any resolution of the Board that, by its express terms, is not so amendable or repealable;

(6) The appointment of other committees of the Board, or of the HC, or their members;

(7) The approval of any self-dealing transaction, as such transactions are by the Georgia Nonprofit Corporation Code.

(b) Any committee must be created, and the members thereof appointed, by resolution adopted by a majority of the authorized number of directors then in office, provided a quorum is present. The Board may appoint, in the same manner, alternate members of any committee who may replace any absent member at any meeting of the committee. The Board shall have the power to prescribe the manner in which proceedings of any such committee shall be conducted. In the absence of any such prescription, such committee shall have the power to prescribe the manner in which its proceedings shall be conducted. Unless the Board or such committee shall otherwise provide, the regular and special meetings and other actions of any such committee shall be governed by the provisions of this Article V applicable to meetings and actions of the Board. Minutes shall be kept of each meeting of each committee.

(c) The Board shall appoint an Audit Committee of the Board consisting of three or more members, a majority of whom shall not be affiliated with any officer of the corporation. The Audit Committee shall and shall have all powers necessary to assure that the corporation's financial affairs are managed in accordance with all applicable laws, and these By Laws.

Section 5.13 Advisory or Operating Committees.

(a) The Board may from time to time appoint advisory or operating committees as deemed appropriate (called "advisory" committees in these Bylaws), consisting of directors or persons who are not directors, or both, but such advisory committees shall not be deemed committees of the Board and shall not exercise any powers of the Board. Notice of, and procedures for, meetings of advisory committees shall be as prescribed by the chairman of each such advisory committee, and meetings of the any advisory committee may be called by the Chairman of the Board, the Board, the Vice Chairman or the chairman of the advisory committee.

An Executive Committee of the HC may be created to coordinate and supervise the activities of the various Divisions of the HC and report their activities to the Board

(b) The HC Board of Governors Advisory Committee may be created to maintain communications with and coordinate activities with each District Leaders that is participating in the HC, to render advice to the HC from the perspective of each of the participating Districts, and to assist the HC in recruiting qualified candidates from all of the participating Districts to assist in various roles in the HC. The Board of Governors Advisory Committee may consist of a class representative, chosen by the Board, for each class of participating District Governors beginning with the Board class of 2010/2011 through the Convention class of 2020/2021.

Section 5.14 Fees and Compensation. Directors and members of committees may receive such compensation, if any, for their services, and such reimbursement for expenses, as may be fixed or determined by the Board.

ARTICLE VI
OFFICERS

Section 6.1 <u>Officers</u>. The officers of this corporation shall be a Chairman of the Board (also called the Chief Executive Officer or CEO), a Vice Chairman (also called the Chief Operating Officer or COO), a Secretary and a Treasurer/CFO (also sometimes called the Chief Financial Officer or CFO). This corporation may also have, at the discretion of the Board, such other officers as may be elected or appointed in accordance with the provisions of Section 6.3 of these Bylaws. Any number of offices may be held by the same person except that neither the Secretary nor the Chief Financial Officer may serve concurrently as Vice Chairman or Chairman of the Board.

Section 6.2 <u>Election</u>. The officers of this corporation shall serve at the pleasure of the Board, and shall hold their respective offices until their resignation, removal, or other disqualification from service, or until such earlier time as their respective successors shall be elected.

Section 6.3 <u>Subordinate Officers</u>. The Board may elect, and the Chairman of the Board may appoint from time to time, such other subordinate officers as the business of this corporation may require, each of whom shall hold office for such period, have such authority and perform such duties as are provided in these Bylaws or as the Board or Chairman of the Board may from time to time determine.

Section 6.4 Removal And Resignation.

(a) Any officer may be removed, either with or without cause, by the Board at any time.

(b) Any officer may resign at any time by giving written notice to this corporation, but without prejudice to the rights, if any, of this corporation under any contract to which the officer is a party. Any such resignation shall take effect at the date of the receipt of such notice or at any later time specified therein and, unless otherwise specified therein, the acceptance of such resignation shall not be necessary to make it effective.

Section 6.5 Vacancies. A vacancy in any office because of death, resignation, removal, disqualification or any other cause shall be filled as it occurs in the manner prescribed in these Bylaws for election or appointment to such office.

Section 6.6 Chairman of the Board. The Chairman of the Board is the general manager and chief executive officer of this corporation and has, subject to the control of the Board, general supervision, direction and control of the business and officers of this corporation. The Chairman of the Board shall preside at all meetings of the Board. The Chairman of the Board has the general powers and duties of management usually vested in the office of a president and general manager of a corporation and such other powers and duties as may be prescribed by the Board.

Section 6.7 Vice Chairman. The Vice Chairman is the chief operating officer of the corporation and, subject to the control of the Board, is responsible for oversight and supervision of all of the operations of the corporation.

If the Chairman of the Board is not present, the Vice Chairman shall preside at all meetings of the Board. The Vice Chairman has the general powers and duties management usually vested in the office of chief operating officer of a corporation and such other powers and duties as may be prescribed by the Board or Chairman of the Board from time to time.

Section 6.8 Secretary. The Secretary shall attend all meetings of the Board and shall keep or cause to be kept, at the principal office or such other place as the Board may order, a book of minutes of all meetings of the Board, and its committees, with the time and place of holding, whether regular or special, and if special, how authorized, the notice thereof given, the names of those present at Board and committee meetings, and the proceedings thereof. The Secretary shall keep, or cause to be kept the original or a copy of this corporation's Articles and Bylaws, as amended to date. The Secretary shall give, or cause to be given notice of all meetings of the Board and any committees thereof required by these Bylaws or by law to be given, shall keep the seal of this corporation in safe custody and shall also have such other powers and duties as may from time to time be assigned to him or her by the Board, the Chairman of the Board or the Vice Chairman.

Section 6.9 Treasurer and Chief Financial Officer. The Treasurer and Chief Financial Officer of this corporation shall keep and maintain, or cause to be kept and maintained, full and accurate accounts of the properties and business transactions of this corporation and shall send or cause to be sent to the Board such financial statements and reports as are by law or these Bylaws required to be sent to them. The Treasurer and Chief Financial Officer shall deposit this corporation's funds and other valuables in the name and to the credit of this corporation with such depositaries as may be designated by the Board. The Treasurer and Chief Financial Officer shall disburse the funds of this corporation as may be ordered by the Board, taking proper vouchers for such disbursements, shall render to the Chairman of the Board, the Vice Chairman and the directors, whenever they request it, an account of all transactions as Treasurer and Chief Financial Officer and of the financial condition of this corporation, and shall have such other powers and perform such other duties as may be prescribed by the Board.

Section 6.10 <u>Duties May Be Delegated</u>. In case of the absence of any officer of this corporation, or for any other reason that the Board may deem sufficient, the Board may delegate, for the time being, all or part of the powers or duties of such officer to any other officer or to any director.

ARTICLE VII
<u>OTHER PROVISIONS</u>

Section 7.1 <u>Amendments</u>. These Bylaws may be amended or repealed by the approval of two-thirds (2/3) of the directors who are then in office at any time.

Section 7.2 <u>Endorsement Of Documents; Contracts</u>. Subject to the provisions of applicable law, any note, mortgage, evidence of indebtedness, contract, conveyance or other instrument in writing and any assignment or endorsement thereof executed or entered into between this corporation and any other person, when signed by the Chairman of the Board or the Vice Chairman and by the Secretary or the Chief Financial Officer of this corporation shall be valid and binding on this corporation in the absence of actual knowledge on the part of the other person that the signing officers had no authority to execute the same. Any such instruments may be signed by any other person or persons and in such manner as from time to time shall be determined by the Board, and, unless so authorized by the Board, no officer, agent or employee shall have any power or authority to bind this corporation by any contract or engagement or to pledge its credit or to render it liable for any purpose or amount.

Section 7.3 Construction And Definitions. Unless the context otherwise requires, the general provisions, rules of construction and definitions contained in the Georgia Nonprofit Corporation Code shall govern the construction of these Bylaws.

Section 7.4 Annual Report. The Board shall cause a written annual report to be sent to the directors within 120 days after the end of this corporation's fiscal year. The annual report shall be accompanied by an financial audit of the corporation for such year prepared in accordance with generally accepted accounting principles and certified by an independent accounting firm.

ARTICLE VIII
INDEMNIFICATION

Section 8.1 Definitions. For the purposes of this Article VIII, "agent" means any person who is or was a director, officer, employee, or other agent of this corporation, or is or was serving at the request of this corporation as a director, officer, employee, or agent of another foreign or domestic corporation, partnership, joint venture, trust, committee, or other enterprise, or was a director, officer, employee, or agent of a foreign or domestic corporation which was a predecessor corporation of this corporation or of another enterprise at the request of such predecessor corporation; "proceeding" means any threatened, pending, or completed action or proceeding, whether civil, criminal, administrative, or investigative; and "expenses" includes, without limitation, attorneys' fees and any expenses of establishing a right to indemnification under Sections 8.4 or 8.5(b) of these Bylaws.

Section 8.2 Indemnification in Actions by Third Parties. This corporation shall have power to indemnify any person who was or is a party or is threatened to be made a party to any proceeding (other than an action by or in the right of this corporation to procure a judgment in its favor, or an action brought by the Attorney General or a person granted relator status by the Attorney General for any breach of duty relating to assets held in charitable trust), by reason of the fact that such person is or was an agent of this corporation, against expenses, judgments, fines, settlements, and other amounts actually and reasonably incurred in connection with such proceeding if such person acted in good faith and in a manner such person reasonably believed to be in the best interests of this corporation and, in the case of a criminal proceeding, had no reasonable cause to believe the conduct of such person was unlawful. The termination of any proceeding by judgment, order, settlement, conviction, or upon a plea of nolo contendere or its equivalent shall not, of itself, create a presumption that the person did not act in good faith and in a manner which the person reasonably believed to be in the best interests of this corporation or that the person had reasonable cause to believe that the person's conduct was unlawful.

Section 8.3 <u>Indemnification in Actions by or in the Right of this Corporation</u>. This corporation shall indemnify, to full extent permitted by law, any person who was or is a party or is threatened to be made a party to any threatened, pending, or completed action related to such person's service as a Board or committee member or officer of this corporation or by reason of the fact that such person is or was an agent of this corporation, against expenses actually and reasonably incurred by such person in connection with the defense or settlement of such action if such person acted in good faith, in a manner such person believed to be in the best interests of this corporation, and with such care, including reasonable inquiry, as an ordinarily prudent person in a like position would use under similar circumstances.

Section 8.4. <u>Indemnification Against Expenses</u>. To the extent that an agent of this corporation has been successful on the merits in defense of any proceeding referred to in Section 8.2 or 8.3 of these Bylaws or in defense of any claim, issue or matter therein, the agent shall be indemnified against expenses actually and reasonably incurred by the agent in connection therewith.

Section 8.5 <u>Insurance</u>. This corporation shall have the power to purchase and maintain insurance on behalf of any agent of this corporation against any liability asserted against or incurred by the agent in such capacity or arising out of the agent's status as such whether or not this corporation would have the power to indemnify the agent against such liability under the provisions of this Article VIII.

APPENDIX C

———◦◦◦❧◈❧◦◦◦———

NY Attorney General's Non-Profit Corporation Guidance

Right From The Start:
Responsibilities of Directors
of Not-for-Profit Corporations

NEW YORK STATE OFFICE

of the

ATTORNEY
GENERAL

Charities Bureau

120 Broadway
New York, NY 10271
(212) 416-8400

www.charitiesnys.com

Right From the Start
Responsibilities of Directors of Not-for-Profit Corporations

Attorney General
of the State of New York
Charities Bureau
120 Broadway
New York, NY 10271

(212) 416-8401
www.charitiesnys.com

New York State Attorney General Eric T. Schneiderman is pleased to offer this booklet to assist current and future boards of directors of New York not-for-profit corporations (and, by analogy, trustees of New York charitable trusts) to understand and carry out their fiduciary responsibilities to the organizations they serve.

Charitable organizations contribute substantially to our society. They educate our children, care for the sick, preserve our literature, art and music for us and future generations, house the homeless, protect the environment and much more. The fiduciaries of those charitable organizations are responsible for managing and preserving the charitable assets that benefit all of us.

Whatever their mission or size, all organizations should have policies and procedures established so that (1) boards understand their fiduciary responsibilities, (2) assets are managed properly and (3) the charitable purposes of the organization are carried out. A failure to meet these obligations is a breach of fiduciary duty and can result in financial and other liability for the board of directors..

Please read this booklet carefully. It contains general information concerning fiduciary oversight of charitable assets. The Attorney General publishes another booklet, *Internal Controls and Financial Accountability for Not-for-Profit Boards*, which contains more detailed information on managing a charitable organization and overseeing its assets. That booklet and other publications of interest to board members may be found at:

www.charitiesnys.com

This booklet is designed to provide guidance to fiduciaries of charitable assets. It is not a substitute for

→ Find out if the organization is required to register with the Attorney General's Charities Bureau and, if so, whether it has registered and filed all required reports. Evaluate whether the filings, audit reports and other compliance requirements appear to be completed on a timely basis. Find out whether there are any tax issues or concerns, or notices received from governmental authorities. Find out what other filings might be required. If the organization has paid employees, it must file the appropriate payroll tax forms and pay the appropriate taxes. The organization may also have sales tax and unrelated business income tax responsibilities.

→ Obtain an understanding of the internal control structure of the organization and the processes in place to monitor it. Determine whether there is a current accounting policies and procedures manual that is followed. Review the past two (2) years, management letters received from the public accountants and find out what has been done to remedy any problems identified. (For further information on internal controls and accountability, please see the Attorney General's Charities Bureau booklet - *Internal Controls and Financial Accountability for Not-for-Profit Boards.* That booklet and other publications of interest to charitable fiduciaries are available at www.charitiesnys.com.

→ Understand the organization's mission, learn about its programs, read its publications, visit its program sites, look at its website and talk to key staff and major donors. Find out about its reputation in the community.

→ Review the organizational chart and understand the accountability structure of the organization. Find out the backgrounds of key management and understand the employee evaluation and compensation processes and due diligence procedures for material contracts entered into.

→ Make sure there is a conflict of interests and code of ethics policy in place and that it is updated annually.

→ Find out what committees the board has established and decide which (if any) to join. Make sure the committees appear to be sufficient (investment, budget, finance, audit, compensation, human resources, nominating, governance, etc.).

→ Determine who the organization's auditors are, what their reputation is and what their performance of the audit process has been.

→ Find out if materials to be considered by the board or its committees are distributed in advance of meetings and whether they provide sufficient information necessary to be part of the stewardship process. Find out how the meetings are structured; by consent agenda or other means.

→ Obtain the current year's budget and cash flow projections. Find out how they compare to actual income and expenses and what processes are in place to monitor these comparisons.

→ Find out whether the insurance coverage appears to be appropriate, including Directors and Officers' liability and employee fidelity insurance. The latter is particularly important - it is surprising how often embezzlement is discovered.

→ Be sure to be able to devote the time expected of a board member. Understand any responsibilities for fundraising, personal giving commitments and other functions expected of board members. Learn what training (if any) is provided to the board. Joining a board without sufficient time to devote to its business is often at the root of troubles faced by many boards. A decision to decline an invitation to join a board because the invited individual is "over-extended" should be respected.

III.   WHAT ARE THE DUTIES OF BOARDS OF DIRECTORS?

While the board is not usually involved in the day-to-day activities of the organization, it is responsible for managing the organization and must make decisions crucial to the life and direction of the organization, such as adding or removing board members, hiring and firing key officers and employees, engaging auditors and other professionals and authorizing significant financial transactions and new program initiatives. In carrying out those responsibilities, members of a board of directors must fulfill fiduciary duties to the organization and the public it serves. Those primary legal duties include the duties of *care, loyalty* and *obedience*. If the organization has affiliates or subsidiaries, the legal duty of impartiality, the duty of fairness to all the charitable interests, may also come into play.

→ Determine who the organization's auditors are, what their reputation is and what their performance of the audit process has been.

→ Find out if materials to be considered by the board or its committees are distributed in advance of meetings and whether they provide sufficient information necessary to be part of the stewardship process. Find out how the meetings are structured; by consent agenda or other means.

→ Obtain the current year's budget and cash flow projections. Find out how they compare to actual income and expenses and what processes are in place to monitor these comparisons.

→ Find out whether the insurance coverage appears to be appropriate, including Directors and Officers' liability and employee fidelity insurance. The latter is particularly important - it is surprising how often embezzlement is discovered.

→ Be sure to be able to devote the time expected of a board member. Understand any responsibilities for fundraising, personal giving commitments and other functions expected of board members. Learn what training (if any) is provided to the board. Joining a board without sufficient time to devote to its business is often at the root of troubles faced by many boards. A decision to decline an invitation to join a board because the invited individual is "over-extended" should be respected.

III. WHAT ARE THE DUTIES OF BOARDS OF DIRECTORS?

While the board is not usually involved in the day-to-day activities of the organization, it is responsible for managing the organization and must make decisions crucial to the life and direction of the organization, such as adding or removing board members, hiring and firing key officers and employees, engaging auditors and other professionals and authorizing significant financial transactions and new program initiatives. In carrying out those responsibilities, members of a board of directors must fulfill fiduciary duties to the organization and the public it serves. Those primary legal duties include the duties of *care*, *loyalty* and *obedience*. If the organization has affiliates or subsidiaries, the legal duty of impartiality, the duty of fairness to all the charitable interests, may also come into play.

→ Determine who the organization's auditors are, what their reputation is and what their performance of the audit process has been.

→ Find out if materials to be considered by the board or its committees are distributed in advance of meetings and whether they provide sufficient information necessary to be part of the stewardship process. Find out how the meetings are structured; by consent agenda or other means.

→ Obtain the current year's budget and cash flow projections. Find out how they compare to actual income and expenses and what processes are in place to monitor these comparisons.

→ Find out whether the insurance coverage appears to be appropriate, including Directors and Officers' liability and employee fidelity insurance. The latter is particularly important - it is surprising how often embezzlement is discovered.

→ Be sure to be able to devote the time expected of a board member. Understand any responsibilities for fundraising, personal giving commitments and other functions expected of board members. Learn what training (if any) is provided to the board. Joining a board without sufficient time to devote to its business is often at the root of troubles faced by many boards. A decision to decline an invitation to join a board because the invited individual is "over-extended" should be respected.

III.   WHAT ARE THE DUTIES OF BOARDS OF DIRECTORS?

While the board is not usually involved in the day-to-day activities of the organization, it is responsible for managing the organization and must make decisions crucial to the life and direction of the organization, such as adding or removing board members, hiring and firing key officers and employees, engaging auditors and other professionals and authorizing significant financial transactions and new program initiatives. In carrying out those responsibilities, members of a board of directors must fulfill fiduciary duties to the organization and the public it serves. Those primary legal duties include the duties of *care*, *loyalty* and *obedience*. If the organization has affiliates or subsidiaries, the legal duty of impartiality, the duty of fairness to all the charitable interests, may also come into play.

A. Duty of Care

The *duty of care* requires a director to be familiar with the organization's finances and activities and to participate regularly in its governance. In carrying out this duty, directors must act in "good faith" using the "degree of diligence, care and skill" which prudent people would use in similar positions and under similar circumstances. In exercising the duty of care, responsible board members should, among other things, do the following:

→ Attend all board and committee meetings and actively participate in discussions and decision-making such as setting of policies. Carefully read the material prepared for board and committee meetings prior to the meetings and note any questions they raise. Allow time to meet without senior management present.

→ Read the minutes of prior meetings and all reports provided, including financial statements and reports by employees. Make sure her or his votes against a particular proposal are completely and accurately recorded. Do not hesitate to suggest corrections, clarification and additions to the minutes or other formal documents.

→ Make sure to get copies of the minutes of any missed committee or board meeting and read them timely, suggesting any changes that may be appropriate.

→ Make sure there is a clear process for approval of major obligations such as fundraising, professional fees (including auditors), compensation arrangements and construction contracts.

→ Make sure that board minutes reflect any dissenting votes in action taken by the board or that any dissenting vote is expressed in writing by letter to the board. Such records are necessary in order for a board member to disclaim responsibility for any particular decision. Absent board members must do this promptly in writing.

→ Read any literature produced as part of the organization's programs.

→ Make sure that monthly financial charts of accounts and financial reports prepared for management are available to the board or finance and audit committees, and that they are clear and communicate proper information for stewardship. Make sure there is an ongoing actual to budget comparison with discrepancies explained.

→ Participate in risk assessment and strategic planning discussions for the future of the organization.

→ Insure that the organization has addressed the sufficiency of its written internal financial controls and written policies that safeguard, promote and protect the organization's assets and that they are updated regularly. Obtain an employees, officers and directors fidelity bond to protect the organization from embezzlement. Have a policy regarding disclosure and identification of fraud (whether or not material). Make sure a policy for records retention and whistleblower protection is in place. Create a background check policy for prospective employees.

→ Determine whether or not the organization indemnifies its officers and directors from liability and has directors' and officers' liability insurance. If it does, find out what is covered and what is not. If it does not, find out why.

→ Encourage diversity among board members. Diversity will help insure a board committed to serve the organization's mission with a range of appropriate skills and interests.

→ Be involved in the selection and periodic review of the performance of the organization's Chief Executive Officer, Chief Financial Officer and other key employees responsible for the day-to-day activities of the organization. The board is responsible for ascertaining whether these individuals have the appropriate education, skills and experience to assume a key position and then evaluating their performance.

B. Duty of Loyalty

The board should have a written "conflicts of interest" policy so that all members are aware of the type of transactions that may prohibit them from joining the board. Some such policies prohibit board members from engaging in any transaction that may result in even the appearance of a conflict of interest. They should provide for written disclosure of anticipated or actual conflicts.

Directors are charged with the duty to act in the interest of the corporation. This duty of loyalty requires that any conflict of interest, real or possible, always be disclosed in advance of joining a board and when they arise. Board members should avoid transactions in which they or their family members benefit personally. If such transactions are unavoidable, disclose them fully and completely to the board.

In order to exercise this *duty of loyalty* directors must be careful to examine transactions that involve board members or officers. The board must not approve any transaction that is not fair and reasonable, and a conflicted board member may not participate in the board vote. There should be an established code of ethics in place that is updated annually as well.

Transactions involving conflicts should be fully documented in the board's minutes, and conflicts policies and disclosure statements should be discussed with the organization's auditors and attorneys.

C. Duty of Obedience

A board has a *duty of obedience* to insure that the organization complies with applicable laws and regulations and its internal governance documents and policies, including:

→ Dedicating the organization's resources to its mission.

→ Insuring that the organization carries out its purposes and does not engage in unauthorized activities.

→ Complying with all appropriate laws, including registering with the Attorney General's Charities Bureau in New York State, complying with registration and reporting laws and other applicable laws of all states in which it conducts activities and\or solicits contributions, filing required financial reports with the Attorney General, the State Worker's Compensation Board, the State Department of Taxation and Finance and the Internal Revenue Service, paying all taxes such as Social Security, income tax withholding (federal, state and local) and any unrelated business income tax. Board members may be personally liable for failing to pay employees' wages and benefits and withholding taxes on employees' wages.

→ Providing copies of its applications for tax-exempt status (IRS Form 1023), federal reports (IRS forms 990, 990 PF, 990 EZ) and its financial reports filed with the Attorney General's Charities Bureau to members of the public who request them.

IV.   IDENTIFY, UNDERSTAND AND UPDATE THE ORGANIZATION'S MISSION AND
        INTERNAL POLICIES

Nonprofit organizations are created to achieve a specific purpose or purposes, such as making grants to operating charities, setting up a soup kitchen, teaching children to read, providing health care, supporting cultural institutions, preserving the environment, assisting senior citizens or one of the many thousands of other charitable activities conducted in our state and our country. Those purposes, or the mission of the organization, are described in the organization's certificate of incorporation and\or by-laws or other constituent document.

If an organization's purposes are not already clearly stated in one of its organizational documents, one of the first activities of the board should be to draft a clear statement of the organization's mission (which should correspond to its stated purpose to the IRS) and to ensure that everyone involved with the organization, directors and officers, employees, volunteers, fundraising professionals, and other professionals, is fully familiar with and understands the mission. Those individuals plan its future, conduct its programs, raise its funds, make it known to the public, present its financial records to regulatory agencies and others and give it professional advice. Unless they fully understand why the organization was formed and what it plans to accomplish, they will not be able to perform their respective tasks appropriately. The mission should be periodically re-assessed and evaluated and amended as needed.

Employees and volunteers should be aware of the organization's internal controls that impact their area of responsibility. At the time of adoption or revisions of internal controls, all directors, officers, employees and volunteers should be made aware of the organization's internal controls, given a copy of the policy and procedures manual, and trained to understand what is expected of them in carrying out their duties and in advising the organization's management and\or the board of directors of violations of the policy. New employees and volunteers should be trained before they assume their responsibilities.

Periodic review of an organization's structure, procedures and programs will assist board members in determining what is working well and what practices the organization might want to change in order to be more efficient, effective or responsible.

V.   MONITOR FUNDRAISING CONDUCTED ON BEHALF OF THE ORGANIZATION

Many organizations contract with professionals to raise funds on their behalf. Since the fund raiser represents the organization to the public, the selection of a fund raising professional is extremely important. Establishing and following procedures for selection of a fund raising professional can avoid future problems. Such procedures should include:

→ Obtaining bids from several fundraising professionals before entering into a contract. Services and fees differ, and comparing bids will aid in the selection of the best contractor for the organization.

→ Checking with the Attorney General's Charities Bureau to see if the fundraising professional being considered are registered and have filed all required contracts and financial reports.

→ Asking the Charities Bureau for copies of the fundraising professional's contracts with other charities to determine the services performed for and the fees charged to those charities.

→ Asking the fundraising professional for references. A reputable fund raising professionals should be happy to provide a potential client with the names, addresses and telephone numbers of some of its clients.

→ Contacting some of the fundraising professional's other clients to see if those nonprofits were satisfied with the services received.

→ Finding out whether the organization's fundraising contracts contain the clauses required by Article 7-A of the Executive Law.

→ Reviewing all written solicitations and scripts used by the fund raising professional, making sure that solicitation material appropriately describes the organization and its activities, includes the name of the organization as registered with the Attorney General and advises potential contributors that they may obtain the organization's financial report from the organization itself or from the Attorney General.

→ Requiring, as mandated by New York law, that the fundraising professional and any of its representatives ("professional solicitors") disclose the name of the specific professional solicitor and the employing fundraising professional and state that the solicitor is being paid to raise funds.

VI.   MAKE USE OF AVAILABLE RESOURCES

In carrying out their responsibilities, board members should realize that they need not do it alone. There are may resources available to assist not-for-profit organizations in fulfilling their fiduciary duties. Following are some of those resources:[1]

The Attorney General's Web site - http://www.charitiesnys.com - posts all forms and instructions for registration and annual filing with the Charities Bureau, links to other web sites that provide resources for not-for-profit boards and publications of interest to not-for-profit organizations.

If the material on the Attorney General's web site does not answer your particular question, you may make an inquiry to the Charities Bureau by phone or email.

---

[1] In addition to the resources listed in this booklet, many more resources are available on the Internet and in communities around the state. Inclusion of any particular entity should not be construed as an endorsement of that entity or the services it renders.

About the Author

---∘∘∘❋∘∘∘---

F. T. Davis, Jr. has successfully chaired non-profit boards of all types, from public charities, to government groups at the federal, state and local level, and has advised boards and board leaders of all types as their legal counsel for many years. He holds degrees from Princeton and Harvard Universities, and has specialized in governance matters for businesses, non-profits, and government.

www.ingramcontent.com/pod-product-compliance
Lightning Source LLC
Chambersburg PA
CBHW031519270326
41930CB00006B/440